THE SIMULATION UNPLUGGED

THE SIMULATION UNPLUGGED

A CRITICAL ASSESSMENT OF NICK BOSTROM'S SIMULATION ARGUMENT

SASHA ZOUEV

THE NEW COLLEGE OF THE HUMANITIES
MA PHILOSOPHY 2020
DISSERTATION

ZOUEV PUBLISHING
NW8 9PA, London
www.zouevpublishing.com

ISBN 978-1-9163451-2-6

First published as part of a Master of Philosophy postgraduate dissertation thesis at the New College of the Humanities, London

Copyright © Sasha Zouev 2020
This book is printed on acid-free paper.

Contact:
Alexander (Sasha) Zouev
Alexander.Zouev@gmail.com
0044 7710836424

TABLE OF CONTENTS

1. INTRODUCTION 9
1.2 TERMINOLOGY 10
1.3 WHY IS THIS IMPORTANT? 14
1.4 WHAT IS THIS PAPER ABOUT? 16
1.5 WHAT IS THIS PAPER NOT ABOUT? 18

2. ASSUMPTIONS 19
2.1 THE METAPHYSICAL ASSUMPTION: SIMULATED CONSCIOUSNESS 19
2.2 THE EMPIRICAL ASSUMPTION: TECHNOLOGICAL LIMITS 24

3. THE SIMULATION ARGUMENT [SA] 32
3.1 FROM SIMULATION ARGUMENT TO SIMULATION HYPOTHESIS 40
3.2 PROBLEMS WITH BOSTROM'S SIMULATION ARGUMENT 43
3.3 A SIMPLIFIED (ANTHROPOCENTRIC) SIMULATION ARGUMENT 53

4. INTERPRETATION OF THE SA 62

4.1 OUTCOME 1 – ALMOST ALL CIVILIZATIONS FAIL TO REACH A POSTHUMAN STAGE 62

4.2 OUTCOME 2: ALL CIVILIZATIONS LOSE INTEREST IN RUNNING SIMULATIONS 67

4.3 OUTCOME 3 – WE ARE ALMOST DEFINITELY IN A COMPUTER SIMULATION 70

4.4 A DEPARTURE FROM TRADITIONAL SCEPTICISM 74

4.5 ON TESTING THE SIMULATION HYPOTHESIS . 78

5. CONCLUSION 80

REFERENCED READINGS 82
APPENDIX A: FIXING THE BUG IN THE SIMULATION 91
APPENDIX B: USING DENSITIES FOR AN INFINITE UNIVERSE 103
APPENDIX C: EXAMINER FEEDBACK 105

1. INTRODUCTION

This book will provide a critical assessment of the simulation argument as presented in a short 2003 paper by philosopher Nick Bostrom entitled '*Are You Living in a Computer Simulation?*' Therein, Bostrom argues that at least one of these statements must be true:

[P1] Almost all civilizations will not reach a posthuman stage.

[P2] Almost all posthuman civilizations will have no interest in making ancestor simulations.

[P3] We are almost definitely living in a computer simulation.

The above can be restated as a tripartite disjunction[1]: [P1] V [P2] V [P3]. It therefore follows that unless we are in a computer simulation right now, the likelihood of us ever reaching a posthuman stage where we run ancestor simulations is negligibly small.

---

[1] Disjunction simply means that the argument is true if at least one of the disjuncts ([P1] or [P2] or [P3]) is true, and false otherwise. Tripartite means there are three statements of alternatives.

The structure of this book is as follows. Section 1 will introduce key concepts and explain why the simulation argument is worth our philosophical attention. Section 2 evaluates the two assumptions underlying Bostrom's argument. Section 3 presents a formal mathematical exposition of the simulation argument. This section also discusses several problems with the argument and suggests how they can be overcome by proposing a modification. Section 4 looks at each outcome and discusses how we should best interpret them. I then argue that Bostrom is wrong to assign equal credence to each outcome. Instead, I suggest that outcome [P1] should be given preference because it requires the least amount of speculation and additional assumptions. I conclude by agreeing with Bostrom that the simulation hypothesis, however unlikely, is fundamentally different from other well-known scepticism scenarios.

1.2 TERMINOLOGY

Before proceeding to present the formal basis for the argument, we need to properly explain some of Bostrom's terminology. A *simulation* (more specifically, a computer simulation) is the reproduction of some process or system using computation. For example, on your computer, you are likely to find a simulation of the card game Solitaire. We can also simulate things like weather, economic forecasts, or how CO_2 emissions affect global temperatures. In the context of Bostrom's argument, the simulation could be a virtual model replica of our civilization.[2] Virtual here indicates that the contents of the simulation do not physically exist but are created by the software. The software is the program used by the computer that is in charge of processing the information. These simulations, although virtual, are to be thought of in a literal sense.[3]

The computers needed to run these simulations would need to be substantially larger and have more memory and processing power than our regular desktop computers. However, the computer does not have to strictly resemble a computer as we think of one today. There is also the possibility that the simulation could be run on quantum computers, or some kind of future computing system which we have not yet developed.[4] A computer simulation is therefore just the use of some computation and technology to simulate another system.[5]

---

[2] It can also be that the simulators are interested in simulating a *process* (such as evolution or a historical event) and for this purpose, they would also require a simulation.

[3] We are not referring to the simulated universe as a kind of metaphor for a processing system. There is a literal simulation that is being run.

[4] Quantum computers approach computation in a fundamentally different way using quantum processes. The problem-solving potential of quantum computers is believed to be substantially faster and more efficient than regular computers.

[5] To better conceptualize these computer simulations, it might help to think of some modern examples of simulation-type video games, such as *The Sims*. It is not hard to imagine that in the distant future, the graphics and

Bostrom's argument also introduces the notion of a *posthuman* race which would be able to run these simulations. Posthuman is a concept borrowed from futurology literature which means a civilization that has reached full technological maturity. More specifically, in another paper, Bostrom (2008: 15) defines a posthuman individual as a person who has gone beyond the "maximum attainable capacities by any current human being without recourse to new technological means." For example, in the future we can expect posthumans to greatly exceed the maximum cognitive capacities, such as memory and general intelligence. The idea of attaining a posthuman status is related to the above discussion of technological ability. Since we currently lack the technology to run these simulations, we are obviously not posthuman.

There is an implicit assumption that a posthuman civilization would have enough computing power to run incredibly detailed simulations while using only a small fraction of their resources for that purpose. As I will discuss in section 2.2, a key characteristic of a posthuman civilization in order for Bostrom's argument to work is its ability to run these ancestor simulations which are detailed enough that the observers within it are fully conscious. Consciousness is a notoriously difficult concept to define. In section 2.1, I will evaluate the assumption that consciousness can be simulated. For now, it would

---

complexity of a game like *The Sims* could allow gamers to simulate environments not too different from our reality.

be best to think of consciousness as the subjective experience of what it is like to be me, or you. The simulation argument thus presupposes that there will come a time where we will be able to simulate consciousness using computation.

An *ancestor simulation* is simply a simulation of the forebearers of a civilization. We can envisage a scenario where if there are indeed posthuman civilizations in the distant future, and if they have the computational power to run detailed simulations, they may well want to simulate life as it was thousands of years ago. This could be for a multitude of reasons such as an interest in our evolutionary history, or a curiosity into how alternate timelines would have played out if certain key events happened or did not happen. In that case, a simulation of our civilization would be an ancestor simulation. As we shall see in section 3.1, Bostrom's argument is open to the possibility of there being many civilizations like ours, scattered throughout our universe. A portion of those civilizations may reach a posthuman status. Each one may then choose to run such ancestor simulations (each of their own forebearers). Posthuman civilizations could have multiple computers running thousands of ancestor simulations of the whole history of humankind.

The *simulation argument* is the tripartite disjunction stated in the introduction. It is the argument that at least one of those three stated propositions must be true. The simulation argument should not be confused with the *simulation hypothesis,* which is the hypothesis that we are currently living in a computer simulation.[6] The simulation argument merely purports to show that one of the three propositions is true (the third of which is the simulation hypothesis). It should be noted that the simulation argument does not imply the simulation hypothesis as its conclusion.

1.3 WHY IS THIS IMPORTANT?

The simulation argument carries a great deal of philosophical importance because it places an interesting constraint on our place in the universe. For philosophers in particular, the third proposition is of most intrigue.[7] The hypothesis that we could be living in a computer simulation is, in some ways, analogous to traditional scepticism thought-experiments such as Descartes' Evil Demon, or the Brain-in-a-Vat scenario. However, as I will cover in section 4.4, the argument that we might be living in a simulation is fundamentally different than

---

[6] If we are in a simulation, then that means the universe is fundamentally computational. However, it is not true that if the universe is computational, that must mean that we are in a simulation. Thus, the simulation hypothesis should not be confused with a form of pancomputationalism (or naturalist computationalism) – which is the view that our entire universe is a computational machine.

[7] It is not just philosophers who are interested in the simulation argument. In 2016, the Bank of America sent out a brief to their clients that estimated a '20%-50% chance that we are living in a simulation' (Udland, 2016)

those traditional scepticism scenarios. This is because the simulation argument, unlike BIV or Descartes' Demon, is a statistical argument. If one finds the simulation argument difficult to refute (as I do), then it does tell us something profound about our world, and we reach this rather extraordinary conclusion using only some basic empirical assumptions. It is not often that such a short philosophical argument exerts this much leverage.

The simulation argument is also a topic that has been popularized (and often mischaracterized) in various media. Simulated universes are a popular trope in science fiction works with perhaps the most famous portrayal being in *The Matrix* trilogy. In recent years, people like Elon Musk, Julian Baggini, and Neil deGrasse Tyson have come out strongly in favour of the simulation argument, and this has rekindled interest in the subject. In this book I intend to steer the conversation away from the pop-science discussions, and back to a more serious academic exploration of the philosophical issues involved. Lastly, for atheists like myself, the simulation argument is perhaps the most persuasive argument for the existence of some kind of 'creator'. If one accepts the premises of the argument, it can certainly tempt even the most devout unbelievers into a mild form of agnosticism.[8] For

---

[8] Richard Dawkins and Sam Harris have both mentioned in various interviews that the simulation hypothesis is something that they take to be a serious possibility (Lee, 2019: 783)

these reasons I think the simulation argument deserves our philosophical interests.

1.4 WHAT IS THIS PAPER ABOUT?

This paper will be focused primarily on Bostrom's original simulation argument. I will address the following questions:

1. How strong are the assumptions needed for the simulation argument?

There are two crucial assumptions which underlie Bostrom's argument. The first is that mental states can be functionally reduced and that computers can give rise to conscious experience. The other is that it is technologically possible to run such immensely detailed and incredibly complex computer simulations. Both of these assumptions will be assessed and also addressed in light of the developments in the 20 years since Bostrom's original paper.

2. What is the core of the simulation argument?

I will show how to set up Bostrom's trilemma using some elementary calculus and probability theory. I will also address the problems with the original formulation and how they can be 'patched' up. The bland indifference principle will be discussed to show why our credence in the hypothesis that we are in a computer simulation should be equal to the proportion of simulated civilizations in our universe.

3. Could I be living in a computer simulation?

Finally, I will consider how we should think about each one of the three outcomes of the simulation argument, with a particular emphasis on the third. I will also discuss how the simulation hypothesis differs from traditional scepticism scenarios.

1.5 WHAT IS THIS PAPER NOT ABOUT?

Bostrom's original paper garnered a rich response of scholarly commentaries and follow-up studies.[9] Given the limited scope of this investigation, there is little opportunity to delve deeper into some of the philosophical issues associated with the simulation argument.[10] The simulation argument has been used as a tool to explore problems in other areas of philosophy including metaphysics (Chalmers 2003; Beisbart 2014; Bostrom 2007), ethics (Dainton 2003; Barrow 2007; Hanson 2001), philosophy of religion (Steinhardt 2010; Crawford 2013; Crummett, 2020), and studies in AI (Ćirković 2015; Virk 2019; Gouveia 2020) Unfortunately, the constraints of this essay mean that we will not be able to explore this additional literature. Moreover, as this is a philosophy essay, I will focus primarily on the philosophical elements, rather than the literature associated with futurism and technology.

---

[9] Many of these papers can be found as a collection on Bostrom's own website; www.simulation-argument.com

[10] A wonderful compilation of academic papers exploring some of these associated issues can be found in GRAU, C. ed. *Philosophers Explore the Matrix*. Oxford University Press on Demand, 2005; and also, IRWIN, W, ed. *The Matrix and Philosophy: Welcome to the Desert of The Real*. Open Court Publishing, 2002.

2. ASSUMPTIONS

2.1 THE METAPHYSICAL ASSUMPTION: SIMULATED CONSCIOUSNESS

Before presenting his simulation argument, Bostrom makes two important assumptions. The first is that of substrate independence. 'Substrate' is a term used to denote the surface material on which some kind of activity occurs. For example, the substrate of our brain activity would be the biological matter (the neuronal cells that make up the brain). 'Independence' in this context means it does not matter what that material is. The term 'substrate independence' is therefore the simple idea that our mental states can reside on a multitude of substrates:

> Mental states can supervene on any of a broad class of physical substrates. Provided a system implements the right sort of computational structures and processes, it can be associated with conscious experiences. It is not an essential property of consciousness that it is implemented on carbon-based biological neural networks inside a cranium: silicon-based processors inside a computer could in principle do the trick as well. (Bostrom, 2003: 2)

There are several terms here that we need to unpack. Within the philosophy of mind, a commonly held position is that of physicalism. Physicalism can best be understood as a metaphysical thesis about what makes up our world. It is metaphysical because it concerns the nature of reality and the relationship between mind and matter. In simple terms, the doctrine of physicalism states that everything is physical. To mean that something is physical is to mean that it is something that the subject of physics is concerned with. This understanding of physicalism thus extends beyond simply material matter and includes things such as forces and mental states.[11] Physicalism claims that the actual world and everything inside it can be exhaustively expressed in physical terms.[12] A more formal definition of physicalism, and one that incorporates the notion of supervenience, is given by Stoljar (2010): "physicalism is the thesis that everything is physical, or as contemporary philosophers sometimes put it, that everything supervenes on, or is necessitated by, the physical."

---

[11] Although the two terms are often used interchangeably, physicalism and materialism are not quite the same. Physicalism is an updated version of materialism – one that considers our current understanding of physics and that the world is not just made up of material things like tables and chairs.

[12] This is not to say that physics posits these mental states. Rather, it posits things like particles and forces (and with these we can in principle explain everything else).

Therefore, ultimately, physicalists insist that even non-material, non-physical things (such as consciousness) would *supervene* on the physical.[13] If physicalism is true, then there can be no difference in how things are without a physical difference. For example, if you went from feeling happy to suddenly feeling sad, a physical change must have occurred in your brain chemistry. Thus, if the mental facts could not be different without the physical facts being different, then we can say that the mental *supervenes* on the physical.[14] Bostrom (2003: 2) does admit that this assumption of substrate independence is "not entirely uncontroversial" however that it is "commonly held within the philosophy of mind".[15] It is also a popular view in modern neuroscience that you are the sum total of all the pieces of your brain and that there is a vastly complicated network of neurons (of which there are over 100bn neurons) and each has over 10,000 connections (von Bartheld et al., 2016). Despite the elaborate complexity of this system, it is still fundamentally a purely physical system.

---

[13] Reframing physicalism in terms of supervenience has been customary since Davidson (1970).

[14] The use of the word 'mental' here just refers to the mental state that a person or agent is in.

[15] Note that this assumption is not universally accepted amongst philosophers: For example. biologist and philosopher M. Pigliucci rejects the idea that consciousness is substrate-independent (Pigliucci, 2013).

Bostrom claims that if consciousness is something that arises from brain states, then if we were able to simulate the human brain down to the level of individual neurons, the simulation itself should give rise to conscious experience. If we have the ability to create simulations with that level of detail and granularity (down to the individual synapses) then the simulation itself should create consciousness. Hypothetically, we should be able to take the physical stuff of the brain and reproduce its software on other substrates – for example, an artificial brain made of aluminium. It is also possible that we could reproduce that brain activity in silico.[16] The computational challenges of simulating consciousness cannot be underestimated as we shall see in the following section. For now, we are merely concerned with the assumption that it *would be theoretically possible* to do so.

Bostrom's (2003: 3) claim that this 'attenuated version of substrate-independence' is something that is 'widely accepted' is a claim that is very difficult to verify[17], and even if we were able to, it would mean little unless we were able to provide concrete reasons as to *why* substrate independence is a commonly held and defensible view –

---

[16] This is an expression which means performed on computer chips (alluding to the silicon used).

[17] Perhaps the closest thing we have to a referendum on this matter is the 2010 PhilPapers survey, in which 57% opted to 'accept or lean towards physicalism' when asked 'physicalism or non-physicalism?'

something that Bostrom himself does not do particularly well.[18] For instance, even if one accepts the substrate independence thesis, Bostrom still needs to answer the question of *how* exactly consciousness would 'spark up' in a simulation.[19] Even if we have computations in the simulation that are identical to computations in a human brain, it seems difficult to conceptualize how consciousness would arise even though the argument does make sense.

Therefore, it is perhaps a bit presumptuous of Bostrom to assume that consciousness can be simulated conditional on the assumption of substrate independence. This assumption is not without its critics. Some philosophers (Searle, 1984; Seth, 2009) and even some neuroscientists (Damasio, 1999) have argued that there is *something* about consciousness that might not be reproducible with computation. For the purposes of this essay however, it is best to grant Bostrom this assumption because an in-depth discussion of simulated artificial consciousness would fall far beyond the scope of this investigation. Substrate independence may not be precisely true, but the assumption

---

[18] Simply claiming that it is a popular view and therefore we should accept it is an appeal to authority. The fact that it is not universally accepted among philosophers indicates that there are persuasive arguments against it.

[19] In personal correspondence, Professor Bostrom has indicated to me that he finds Chalmers (1993) paper '*A Computational Foundation for the Study Of Cognition*' to be a convincing argument as to how suitable structural properties can give rise to consciousness.

is 'true enough' that we can confidently say that brain emulation would give rise to conscious experiences indistinguishable from human ones on biological substrates.

2.2 THE EMPIRICAL ASSUMPTION: TECHNOLOGICAL LIMITS

The second assumption required concerns our actual technical ability to run these highly detailed computer simulations of reality while only using a small fraction of available resources for that purpose. Almost 20 years after Bostrom's paper was first published, our current technological state is not even remotely close to being able to simulate the human brain, let alone an entire civilization. However, many futurologists including Bostrom (1998), Moravec (1999) and Drexler (1985) have presented powerful arguments that in the future we may reach a stage where we would be able to have access to posthuman technological capabilities. We have good empirical evidence to assume that phenomena like Moore's law can also be applied to our computational ability. [20] If we assume that technological progress

---

[20] Moore's law concerns the empirical relationship between the amount of transistors in a circuit and time. The law (or rather observation) roughly states that the transistors *double* every two years. Advancements in other areas of technology (such as memory, and graphics) have been strongly linked to Moore's law. Interestingly, something like the cost of sequencing the human genome has (up until recently) closely followed Moore's law.

continues in a similar pattern, we may one day have access to the necessary technology to run ancestor simulations.

Computational Limits

Bostrom (2003: 3) claims that once we reach a posthuman stage, it will be "possible to convert planets and other astronomical resources into enormously powerful computers" and as a result "it is currently hard to be confident in any upper bound on the computing power that may be available to a posthuman civilization". On the Kardashev scale, we are still a type I planetary civilization.[21] Thus, there is still lots of potential for exploiting potential energy sources. The Matryoshka brain, for example, is a hypothetical megastructure that consists of parts of material that orbit a star that feeds off radiation. It could, in theory, be used to power a computer the size of a planetary star. Bradbury (2001) roughly estimates that a computer of that size would be able to perform operations of up to 10^{42} operations per second. That would give it enough power to simulate hundreds of

---

For more, see HAYDEN, Erika Check. "The $1,000 genome." *Nature* 507.7492 (2014): 294.

[21] In 1964, soviet astronomer Kardashev created a scale to classify levels of civilizations based on how much energy they can extract; A type-I civilization is limited to only the energy on its *planet*. Type-II can harvest planetary systems, and Type III could potentially control energy of the entire galaxy. See Kardashev (1964).

thousands of civilizations at the same time. Drexler (1992) also describes a crude design for a computer model which would be the size of a sugar cube but could perform operations at millions of times the speed of a human brain.

There is also the very real possibility that we discover new technology that is a significant departure from our current conception of computers, and thus we might need to completely rethink our upper bounds. Bostrom (2003: 3) notes that "we could create quantum computers or learn to build computers out of nuclear matter or plasma" and this in turn should push us much closer to the theoretical limits. We have a relatively high degree of confidence that there will be breakthroughs and advancements in things like molecular nanotechnology and space colonization in the near future. As a result, it is possible that there are physical phenomena that would surpass whatever current computational constraints we now envisage as our upper bounds. For example, in June 2020, researchers seemed to find strong evidence that black holes could be used for energy.[22] This is a theory that was first postulated by Roger Penrose, who argued that advanced alien civilizations would harness the power of black holes (Penrose, 1971). Such interventions coupled with quantum computing (and the involvement of AI) could very well cause a significant departure from Moore's law in the sense that we will see even more radical breakthroughs in the near future.

---

[22] See DRINKWATER, B.W. An acoustic black hole. *Nat. Phys.* (2020).

Processing Power

We can also estimate how much computing power would be required to simulate a human mind by looking at how powerful the brain is. On one estimate, the human brain can process about 10^{15} operations per second (Kurzweil, 1999). If that is the amount of power required to experience subjective reality for one person, then we can assume that that is what would be roughly required to simulate a human mind. To simulate *all* the minds that ever existed would be that amount multiplied by 110 billion.[23] Perhaps a better approach would be to look at how much computational power would be required to simulate 10 billion human brains in real time, which some have estimated as 10^{25} operations per second (Sandberg, 2008).[24] Once we start to factor in simulating the rest of the universe, that number of operations starts to get astronomically large. However, there are corners that can be cut with regards to simulating all of reality. As Bostrom notes:

> Simulating the entire universe down to the quantum level is obviously infeasible, unless radically new

---

[23] 110bn is a rough estimate of all humans who have ever lived (from the Population Reference Bureau),

[24] Perhaps that is not an entirely accurate way of approaching the problem since as soon as a simulated person 'dies', we would no longer be required to simulate their brain.

physics is discovered. But in order to get a realistic simulation of human experience, much less is needed – only whatever is required to ensure that the simulated humans, interacting in normal human ways with their simulated environment, do not notice any irregularities. (Bostrom, 2003: 5)

Indeed, it would not be necessary to simulate the entire universe down to each individual atom. Like most modern-day computer games, details could be 'rendered in' in an ad-hoc fashion.[25] For example, when looking at this printed out book, a simulation would only need to include the visual aspects and some macroscopic properties like weight and texture in order to convince you that you are holding paper pages. If you were to inspect the pages more carefully (perhaps under a microscope) then the simulation could fill in additional details.[26] These kinds of simplifications would greatly lessen the computation required

---

[25] Rendering refers to the process of synthesizing images to generate 3D models. Recent developments in video game graphics allow developers to use rendering 'tricks' to give off the illusion of something.

[26] Interestingly, this might help explain a big mystery in quantum physics where the state of a particle is not known until an observation has been made. This would be the case if details are only rendered in when required.

Sensory Details

It is also important that the simulation is able to convince the simulated observers that they are not in a simulation. We want the simulation to be indistinguishable from reality. Given just how incredibly quickly computer graphics have improved over the last 40 years, it is not difficult to imagine that we will have perfect photorealistic graphics in the near future. For example, the game *Pong* was released in 1972 and consisted of essentially two moving pixel blocks simulating the game of table tennis. Today, the most popular video games are getting remarkably close to being photorealistic representations. Moreover, recent developments in Virtual Reality gaming seem to indicate that already we are able to 'fool' gamers into believing that a virtual world is real. Of all the aspects covered in this section, developing real-life graphics is perhaps the least controversial.

A common error when discussing this assumption is to introduce an unnecessary time constraint. While it is true that currently we are not particularly close to being able to simulate civilizations to the required level of detail, the timeframe does not really matter for the simulation argument as long as technological progress continues. This technological assumption places no constraint on *when* we are able to run these simulations. The only thing that matters is that at some point in the future we will have this capacity. Whether that happens in 100 or 10,000 years does not really matter.[27]

Obstacles to Modelling

It is evident that modelling the entire universe as a simulation is an incredibly difficult undertaking, and some recent research has started to ask whether it is even physically possible. In 2017, a pair of researchers from the University of Oxford published a paper which tried to argue that it is actually impossible that we are living in a simulation.[28] Ringel and Kovrizhin (2017) found that it would be impossible to simulate at least one aspect of the universe – something known as the quantum Hall effect (which describes the way electrons bounce between energy states in a quantum leap). The researchers found that to accurately simulate the effect, the computational power would need to *double* each time you introduce a new particle into the model. Upon adding just a few hundred particles, the operations per second required grows to a number that is greater than the number of atoms there are in the universe. The result is that it would be impossible to have that many operations, even with some of the

---

[27] This is only *partly* true as we will discuss in section 4.1. The longer we take to develop this technology, the more time we have for our civilization to collapse through some doomsday scenario. Thus, timeframe does not matter but only so long as we (and all other civilizations) do not annihilate ourselves in that time.

[28] See Ringel et al. (2017).

supercomputers proposed earlier. Nonetheless, this finding only indicates that computing in the traditional sense would make it impossible to simulate our universe.[29]

Although we can be fairly optimistic that technological progress will continue, this assumption of posthuman technological capabilities is not accepted by everyone. One might argue that what we are seeing now in terms of technological progress is simply a period of boomtime, and that it cannot go on forever. Perhaps transhumanist like Kurzweil and Drexler are overly optimistic.[30] Nonetheless, as with the first assumption, there is not much evidence to suggest that it would not be feasible to have the computational power needed to run ancestor simulations in the future. Therefore, in order to proceed with this essay, it would be best to grant Bostrom this assumption whilst being cautious about projecting current rates of increase in computational power into the future.

---

[29] Developments in quantum computing would probably circumscribe this. See Lloyd (2000); Berezin (2007).

[30] For instance, a hundred years ago, many respected futurologists predicted flying cars and high-speed space travel as a common occurrence in the 21st century. This obviously did not happen – and a similar fate might await computational power.

3. THE SIMULATION ARGUMENT [SA]

We are now ready to present the simulation argument in full. With some elementary algebra and probability theory, we can show how Bostrom (2003) arrives at the tripartite disjunct stated in the introduction. First, I introduce some notation (which is borrowed from his paper):[31]

f_P – let this be the *fraction of human civilizations* that make it to a posthuman stage and are able to create ancestor-simulations. For example, let us say there have existed a total of 1000 civilizations. If only 100 of these make it to a posthuman stage, then f_P is 0.10. This effectively means that only 10% of all civilizations have the ability to run ancestor-simulations.

$\bar{N}$ – let this be the *average amount of simulations* that are created by a posthuman civilization. These simulations are of the entire ancestral history of that civilization.[32] We deal with 'average' amounts because we assume that there are multiple posthuman civilizations in total,

---

[31] The first few steps are my own because Bostrom does not make this section particularly clear.

[32] A more intuitive analogy would be to think of it as booting up a virtual world of ourselves where our avatars would be conscious simulated observers. That is what the simulation is modelling.

therefore we can take the average amongst them.[33] For example, if there are only 3 civilizations and they run 5 million, 10 million, and 15 million simulations respectively, then $\bar{N}$ for this universe is 10 million.[34]

$\bar{H}$ – let this be the *average amount of individuals* that have lived prior to the civilization becoming posthuman. For example, if there is only one civilization in existence (ours) and tomorrow we somehow reach a posthuman stage, then $\bar{H}$ would be all the individuals that have lived up until that point (which is roughly 110bn births since the start of the human race). Bostrom assumes that when posthuman civilizations run ancestor simulations, they will be simulating the entire mental history of humankind which is why we require $\bar{H}$.

p – the *amount of civilizations* that reach a posthuman stage (and are thus able to run ancestor simulations).

n – the *amount of civilizations* that do not reach a posthuman stage (and therefore will not run any ancestor simulations).

---

[33] Working with averages does not yield a result that is entirely accurate as we shall see in the following section.

[34] Note that this is the number of *simulations*. The number of *simulated observers* would still require us to multiply by how many observers we are simulating.

The *fraction of observers that are simulated* is:

$$f_{sim} = \frac{(amount\ of\ simulated\ observers)}{(amount\ of\ simulated\ observers + amount\ of\ real\ observers)}$$

The number of *simulated observers per civilization* therefore is $\overline{N} \cdot \overline{H}$ (as each ancestor simulation will contain simulations of all the individual observers that have ever lived). This only occurs in the p type civilizations. So, if we want to get the *total amount of simulated observers in the universe,* we need to multiply by p, the amount of civilizations. This gives us the numerator of the following:

$$= \frac{p\overline{N}\overline{H}}{p\overline{N}\overline{H} + p\overline{H} + n\overline{H}}$$

The denominator here is just the numerator plus the addition of the number of real observers (in both types of civilizations),

$$= \frac{p\overline{N}\overline{H}}{p\overline{N}\overline{H} + \overline{H}[p + n]}$$

If we divide top and bottom by the total amount of civilizations, which is $(p + n)$:

$$f_{sim} = \frac{\frac{p}{(p+n)}\overline{N}\overline{H}}{\frac{p}{(p+n)}\overline{N}\overline{H} + \overline{H}}$$

What is $\frac{p}{(p+n)}$? It is the fraction of human civilizations that make it to a posthuman stage, f_P.

The actual fraction of simulated observers with humanlike experiences is therefore:

$$f_{sim} = \frac{f_P \overline{N} \overline{H}}{f_P \overline{N} \overline{H} + \overline{H}}$$

To better conceptualize the above equation, consider the following diagram:

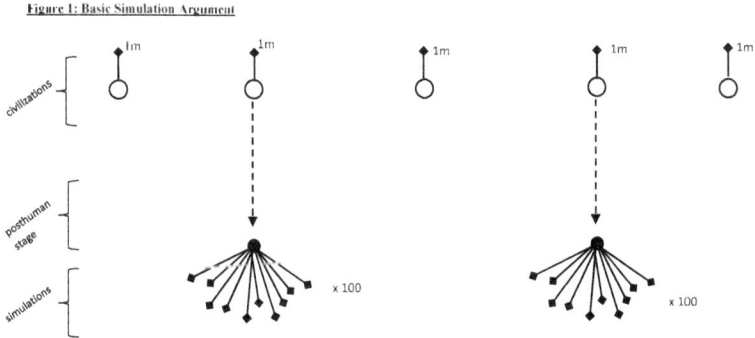

Figure 1: Basic Simulation Argument

In Figure 1, we start with 5 civilizations, each one with 1 million 'real' observers. $\bar{H}$ therefore, is 1m. Of those 5 civilizations, only 2 of them reach a posthuman stage. Thus, $f_P = \frac{2}{5} = 0.4$. At that point they each choose to run 100 ancestor simulations. Therefore, $\bar{N}$ is 100. We now have everything we need to plug into our equation:

$$f_{sim} = \frac{f_P \, \bar{N} \, \bar{H}}{(f_P \, \bar{N} \, \bar{H}) + \bar{H}} = \frac{0.4 \cdot 100 \cdot 1{,}000{,}000}{[0.4 \cdot 100 \cdot 1{,}000{,}000] + 1{,}000{,}000} = \frac{40}{41}$$
$$= 0.9756 \ldots \approx 98\%$$

This means that 98% of all observers in this universe are simulated. Note that if we choose larger values of $\bar{N}$, the value of f_{sim} will tend towards 1. This is understandable because when posthuman civilizations have the technological capabilities to run astronomical amounts of ancestor simulations (in excess of hundreds of millions), then the number of simulated observers will vastly outnumber the 'real' observers.

Bostrom (2003: 7) goes on to argue that perhaps not all civilizations that become posthuman will be interested in creating ancestor simulations. Therefore, we need to introduce some additional notation. Let f_I be the *fraction* of civilizations that have an *interest* in creating these kinds of simulations and let $\bar{N_I}$ be the average amount of simulations that are created by these kinds of interested civilizations. We can now express the following relationship:

$$\overline{N} = f_I \cdot \overline{N_I}$$

This simply means that the average number of simulations that are created by posthuman civilizations is equal to the average number of simulations created by interested civilizations multiplied by the fraction of civilizations that are interested in creating these simulations.

Plugging this in for $\overline{N}$ in our previous equation for f_{sim} we get:

$$f_{sim} = \frac{f_P (f_I \cdot \overline{N_I}) \overline{H}}{(f_P (f_I \cdot \overline{N_I}) \overline{H}) + \overline{H}}$$

We can factor out $\overline{H}$ from both numerator and denominator,

$$f_{sim} = \frac{\overline{H} [f_P f_I \overline{N_I}]}{\overline{H}[(f_P f_I \overline{N_I}) + 1]}$$

Cancelling out and simplifying, we arrive at the final Simulation Argument Formula [SAF]:

$$f_{sim} = \frac{f_P f_I \overline{N_I}}{(f_P f_I \overline{N_I}) + 1}$$

Bostrom (2003: 7) then reasons that due to the enormous computing power that posthuman civilizations will have, $\overline{N_I}$, the average amount of simulations running in the interested civilizations, will be astronomically large.

We can demonstrate what happens with extremely large values of $\overline{N_I}$ by plugging in some example values. Let us assume that $f_P = 0.5$, $f_I = 0.5$, and let $\overline{N_I} = 10,000,000$. We then get:

$$f_{sim} = \frac{(0.5)(0.5)(10,000,000)}{(0.5)(0.5)(10,000,000) + 1} = \frac{2,500,000}{2,500,001} = 0.9999...$$
$$\approx 1$$

Therefore, as it becomes increasingly energy efficient to generate these simulated civilizations, we can expect them to vastly outnumber 'real' civilizations.

As $\overline{N_I}$ tends to a large number, f_{sim} will tend to one.

$$f_{sim} \approx 1$$

This gives us the third proposition from Bostrom's disjunction:[35]

---

[35] These propositions are slightly different from the 3 given in the introduction. We will connect them to probabilities in the following section.

[3] $f_{sim} \approx 1$; the fraction of observers that are simulated is close to 1.

Moreover, a closer inspection of the [SAF] above reveals that the only way for [3] to *not* be the case ($f_{sim} \approx 0$) is if the numerator in the equation tends to zero:[36]

$$f_{sim} = \frac{f_P f_I \overline{N_I}}{(f_P f_I \overline{N_I}) + 1}$$

Therefore, either $f_P \approx 0$, or $f_I \approx 0$, or both tend to zero.

Hence, Bostrom concludes his analysis by noting that *at least one* of these must be the case:

[1] $f_p \approx 0$; the fraction of human civilizations that reach a posthuman stage is almost zero.

[2] $f_I \approx 0$; the fraction of posthumans interested in running simulations is almost zero.

---

[36] By inspecting the SAF, it is evident that f_{sim} will almost always take on a value that is nearly 0 or nearly 1 (getting values of 0.5 or something similar would be an exception).

[3] $f_{sim} \approx 1$; the fraction of all observers in the universe living in a simulation is almost one.

Intuitively, it can indeed be the case that both [1] and [2] are true. For example, if no civilizations reach a posthuman stage ($f_p = 0$) then clearly the fraction of posthuman civilizations with an interest in running these simulations will also be zero ($f_I = 0$).[37]

3.1 FROM SIMULATION ARGUMENT TO SIMULATION HYPOTHESIS

For philosophers, proposition [3] is clearly of most intrigue. We can go one step further from [3] and arrive at the simulation hypothesis [P3] if we utilize what is known as the *bland indifference principle* [BIP].[38] This is a rule which can be used to assign probabilities to epistemic outcomes. Epistemic outcome here simply refers to a statement regarding our knowledge about the world. The BIP states that when we lack any relevant evidence, we should assign credence

---

[37] Of course, we may have civilizations that are interested in running simulations but do not have the capabilities (such as our own). These do not make up f_I because f_I only concerns *posthuman* civilizations.

[38] Bostrom never really explains why this is the *bland* indifference principle. It functions exactly as the regular indifference principle, so I will treat it as such.

(which means our acceptance, or belief) equally across all of the possible outcomes. Assume that some fraction x of observers with humanlike experiences are simulated and that we do not have any further information that might be used as evidence of whether we are simulated or 'real'. Bostrom (2003: 8) argues that in that case, our credence that we are living in a simulation should be x:

$$Cr(SIM|f_{sim} = x) = x$$

Essentially, if we have millions of observers in simulations with identical experiences and also one 'real' universe, the probability that we are in the real one should be equal to that fraction. Therefore, conditional on the truth of [3] $f_{sim} \approx 1$, our credence that we are currently living in a computer simulation should also be close to one (SIM is the thesis that we live in a simulation). For example, if we were to know that 99% of all observers in the universe with our human-like experiences are actually living in a computer simulation then there would be a 99% chance that we ourselves are living in a computer simulation:

$$Cr(SIM|f_{sim} = 0.99) = 99\%$$

An insightful way to think about this is by considering alternative situations in which more and more people live in simulations (90%, 95%, 99.99%, 99.99999% and so on). As you get closer to the limiting case which places *everybody* in the simulation (and so you have to infer that you yourself are in a simulation), the credence assigned to being in a simulation should increase until it approaches complete certainty (Bostrom, 2003: 8). Credence would vary continuously as the underlying fraction varies continuously.

We can make similar transitions (from fractions to credences) for the first two outcomes. If we knew that a fraction ($f_p \approx 0$) fails to reach a posthuman stage, our credence should be that we will also not reach a posthuman stage. And similarly, for the fraction of interested posthumans:

	CONNECTING FRACTIONS TO CREDENCES			
[1] $f_p \approx 0$	The fraction of human civilizations that reach a posthuman stage is almost zero.	[P1]		We will almost definitely fail to reach a posthuman stage.
[2] $f_I \approx 0$	The fraction of posthumans interested in running simulations is almost zero.	[P2]		We will almost definitely not be interested in running ancestor simulations.
[3] $f_{sim} \approx 1$	The fraction of all observers in the universe that are living in a simulation is almost one.	[P3]		We are almost definitely living in a computer simulation.

3.2 PROBLEMS WITH BOSTROM'S SIMULATION ARGUMENT

Although Bostrom's argument is rather elegant in its simplicity, we can identify at least seven important issues. First, there is the 'mathematical non sequitur'[39] that Bostrom himself later noticed (Bostrom and Kulczycki, 2011). Recall that when setting up, we made an initial assumption that civilizations will run simulations *only of their own ancestors*. Yet in the formula, $\bar{H}$ is taken to be the average amount of individuals that lived prior to the civilization reaching a posthuman stage. The SAF therefore depends on the average number of observers in all civilizations and does not differentiate whether they reach a posthuman stage or not. We can envisage scenarios where there might be 100 civilizations like ours with many more 'real' observers, and then only one of those 100 civilizations reaches a posthuman status. If that one civilization had a relatively small pre-posthuman populace, using $\bar{H}$ would not capture the situation correctly, and this can lead to some strange scenarios where all three of Bostrom's propositions are simultaneously false (see Appendix A for a detailed exposition and Bostrom and Kulczycki's proposed solution). To fix this 'bug' in the SAF, we require a further constraint that the average number of observers in the pre-posthuman phase is not significantly larger in non-simulating civilizations than in

---

[39] This means that the conclusion of the argument does not follow from the premises.

civilizations that do end up running ancestor simulations. However, it should also be noted that for sufficiently large $\bar{N}$ (which is something we implicitly assume to be the case), this bug will almost never cause a problem.

Second, it seems rather strange to think that *if* there are indeed other civilizations in the universe, that they would also have human-like observers.[40] We do not really have any evidence that would suggest this to be the case.[41] Even though science-fiction has entrenched in us this idea that other civilizations in the universe would still somehow be inhabited by civilizations with humanlike features, this is wildly speculative. Moreover, the notion that other civilizations with humanlike observers develop in the same way as us is also overly presumptuous. Perhaps our technological progress is unique to our species. If there are other civilizations, there is no guarantee that they have developed computational technology which is similar to ours. Bostrom does not explicitly spell out this assumption, but his argument does seem to rely on some kind of uniformity amongst

---

[40] Of course, it depends exactly what Bostrom means by 'human-like'. I take him to mean almost identical to us, Homo sapiens, and not merely sentient beings.

[41] Even the highly conjectural Drake equation merely estimates that there might be some *communicative* extra-terrestrial life. It tells us nothing about whether the species is human-level or what kind of technology they might possess.

civilizations. It could very well be that the concept of 'simulations' just does not exist in other civilizations. Up until 100 years ago, we did not have computers so the idea of running ancestor simulations was unheard of even for us. It is entirely possible that other human-like civilizations do reach a posthuman level but the ability to run simulations is just something that never develops.

I am also not particularly convinced why Bostrom thinks that if we had the power to run simulations that we would choose to run *ancestor* simulations. It seems more logical that instead of choosing $\bar{H}$ to be all the individuals that have ever lived, we would instead just simulate everyone who is alive at the time that the simulation is booted up.[42] I am not even entirely sure how one would go about simulating our entire history given that we have many gaps to fill when going centuries back (also, where would the simulation start from? The Big Bang? Would dinosaurs be simulated?). Ancestor simulations mean to create a detailed copy of an original example that pre-exists in the 'real world'. Therefore, there is clearly an issue of feasibility when it comes to simulating entire ancestral histories. Of course, the size of $\bar{H}$ does not ultimately change the outcome of the SAF (assuming $\bar{N}$ is large enough), but it is a strange assumption given how most scientific simulations currently work. Similarly,

---

[42] A counterargument here could be that simulating a civilization at a post-human stage would be far more computationally demanding than simulating ancestral histories.

nowhere in Bostrom's equation does he account for the possibility that simulations will be turned off (just like when people stop playing a simulation video game, the simulation ceases to exist). When you have millions of simulations this may not matter much, but if $\bar{N}$ is not sufficiently large, it could drastically change the probability that we are in a simulation (if, for example, the posthumans only keep 3 or 4 simulations running at any time)

Furthermore, Bostrom seems at times to be purposely vague about *what* exactly is being simulated. Consider the title of his paper: '*Are We Living in a Computer Simulation?*' Who exactly is the *we*? It is bizarre to assume that we would be simulated as groups and the simulations would span all of history. Most contemporary simulations in AI are done over a short time frame, and 'sims' are instantiated in games with running time measured in years and not centuries. Unless you can argue that most simulated observers are in long-term, densely populated simulations, then the argument opens up to more sceptical consequences. Although Bostrom tries to avoid speculating too much about the interests of posthumans and what their motivations are (this is covered by [P2]), the fact that his argument centres around *ancestor simulations* means that he is actually making a lot of assumptions. For example, there are many day-to-day activities associated with our world that would be of little interest to posthuman researchers, and it would seem rather pointless to simulate these entirely. Bostrom does not fully acknowledge that unless computational power was near limitless, it would make sense that posthumans diverted these resources to more productive areas.

Similarly, it is possible that not everyone in the simulation will be programmed to have human experiences. Bostrom (2003: 13) does briefly allude to this idea (he calls them 'selective me-simulations', and the rest of humanity as 'shadow people') however he does not acknowledge the impact this would have on $\bar{H}$. Also absent from his brief discussion is the ethical implications of simulating such 'shadow people' as opposed to simulated conscious observers. There is an incredibly good chance that simulations with 'shadow people' may be adequate enough for whatever purposes a posthuman society might have for running the simulation. Also, a fully conscious simulation would likely have some sort of provisions that once it is instantiated, it should never be turned off. This will be more costly to the simulator. Therefore, we may end up with a scenario that is not really covered by any of Bostrom's three outcomes: there are posthumans who are interested in running ancestor simulations and they do so except nobody in the simulation is conscious.[43]

---

[43] It could perhaps be argued that this is covered by [P2] – civilizations will not be interested in running *ancestor simulations* (if one specifies that the ancestor simulations are not conscious). I do think however that this distinction is important insofar that we are certain of our own consciousness.

Third, I take issue with how Bostrom chose to demarcate f_I as the fraction of civilizations that are not *interested* in running simulations. As we shall see in section 4.2, there are actually many reasons (including cost, legality, and computational requirements) as to why posthuman civilizations may not end up creating simulations. Therefore, they can still be interested, but choose not to. Moreover, Bostrom could have just merged [P1] and [P2] into an outcome that essentially says: 'there will be no simulations' (as I will attempt to do in the following section). Instead, he arbitrarily split this up as 'there will be no simulations' because i) it will be impossible or ii) civilizations will not be interested'. But this division seems groundless, or at least Bostrom should have provided some more reasoning. He also could have further split up f_I for the reasons mentioned above (e.g. f_b are civilizations where simulations are banned). This would obviously change the outcomes, and we would no longer have his trilemma. Bostrom does not really provide any justification as to why he separated f_I and f_p as he did.

Fourth, the SAF does not work well if we allow for the concept of infinity (e.g. infinitely many universes, or infinitely many simulations). In this case f_{sim} would be undefined because all of the variables ($\bar{H}$, $\bar{N}$, f_P) in the formula are invalid. As the simulation argument depends heavily on calculating average values across all universes, if there are infinitely many universes, we would have infinity divided by infinity and all of our subsequent calculations would no longer be valid.[44] Bostrom does somewhat address this problem, although not formally.[45] He suggests that we may use a density function, and I expand on the mathematics behind this idea in Appendix B. Then there is also the issue of cardinality.[46] In order to actually calculate f_p, f_I, and f_{sim}, we would require the cardinal set of *all* posthuman civilizations, ancestor simulations, and human level civilizations (Besnard, 2004). Let us call the set of all of these Ω. Even if Ω is not infinite, doing the simple calculations in the way we have in the previous examples is not going to be possible if we do not have the specific numbers of civilizations and simulations.[47] However, one could overcome this issue by looking at the relative sizes. For example, as long as $\bar{N}$ is sufficiently larger than $\bar{H}$, we will still recover the three outcomes of the simulation argument.

---

[44] The simulation hypothesis rests on the idea that there are substantially more simulated observers than real. If we are open to the possibility of infinitely many universes, then this idea breaks down because not all universes will have simulations and therefore it is not for certain that simulated entities outnumber real.

[45] Bostrom does address this as a footnote in the FAQ section of his simulation argument website: https://www.simulation-argument.com/faq.html.

[46] In mathematics, the cardinality of a set is the number of elements in the set.

[47] Of course, Bostrom could counter-argue that we do not necessarily need to know specific numbers – all we really need to know is the relative sizes.

Nonetheless, this is something that Bostrom does not specifically reference in his original paper.

Fifth, it may very well be possible that simulated civilizations themselves become posthuman, and then they in turn also run their own ancestor simulations. In that case we would have 'nested simulations' and this could go on for several levels.[48] Bostrom (2003: 10) only casually notes this as a possibility, without really considering how this affects his argument. Normally, this would vastly increase the average number of simulations ($\bar{N}$). However, there is a caveat we must consider. It could be the case that the base-level simulators would need to expand many more resources once first-level simulations start running simulations of their own (Jenkins 2006: 23). In this case, non-simulated observers may wish to limit the number of simulations they initially run (lowering $\bar{N}$). Some scholars (see Brueckner, 2008, as well as Bostrom's 2009 reply) have questioned whether these nested simulations would really count as *real* simulations because they are created on virtual machines in the simulation. This seems like a rather strange objection to make if one already accepts the assumption of substrate independence (which was needed to make the first simulation possible).

---

[48] Such computers can be thought of as 'virtual machines', which is just a machine simulating another machine.

Sixth, the use of the BIP in Bostrom's reasoning is not entirely uncontroversial. Consider the following analogy: many people throughout history thought that they were Jesus. There has only been one real Jesus. Irrespective of how many people believe that they are Jesus, Jesus's own reasons for thinking he is Jesus are arguably different, and the fact that there are many people who think they are Jesus should not undercut Jesus's confidence. If there were 10,000 people who thought they were Jesus, this does not mean that the real Jesus should only believe he is Jesus with a credence of 1/10,000. One could apply the same logic to simulations. Although we know that there might be millions of simulations that are indistinguishable from our reality, our epistemic situation (the knowledge that we possess about our circumstances) might be different, and we might just *know* that we are not simulated – perhaps because we created the simulations (we will return to this idea in section 3.3). Of course, the Jesus case is not exactly parallel to that of simulations, but it does raise the issue: would sim worlds and real worlds really be that indistinguishable?

Some commentators (see Weatherson, 2003 and the reply from Bostrom, 2005) have tried to argue that we may have some evidence that can be used to update any a-priori credences we have that we might be in a simulation. A-priori here means using theoretical deduction instead of observation or experience. For example, one might reason that it could be the case that our simulators would be more interested in running simulations of important historical periods (like wartime, or key moments like the collapse of the roman empire). Therefore, if we suspect that we are living in a 'special' time, we might interpret this as evidence in support of the simulation hypothesis. However, given the fact that we do not know what the interests of a technologically advanced simulation might be (or if those moments are even important compared to a wide relative history), these kinds of speculations are somewhat futile.

Finally, an interesting paper by Jonathan Birch accuses Bostrom of engaging in a form of *selective scepticism.* Scepticism can be understood as a position that questions whether it is possible to have certainty in knowledge claims.[49] Birch argues that the simulation argument "presupposes that we possess good evidence for claims about the physical limits of computation and yet lack good evidence for claims about our own physical constitution" (Birch, 2013: 3). He essentially argues that in order for the simulation argument to work, we require the same kind of evidence for the two main assumptions as we do for the proposition, 'I have two hands'.[50] Therefore, he is hesitant to accept the argument because he does not think this kind of 'limb scepticism' is justified. Birch then attempts to modify Bostrom's argument in order to defend the position that "although my

---

[49] There are two types of scepticism: academic (knowledge is impossible) and Pyrrhonian (it is not known whether anything can be known).

[50] We will return to this idea in section 4.3 when I discuss why we need both assumptions to be true in order to arrive at outcome [P3], but not [P1].

evidence cannot locate me among the physically real observers, it can establish a *lower bound* on the true physical limits of computations" (Birch, 2013: 12). Ultimately, however, he finds that this defense is also unsuccessful.

3.3 A SIMPLIFIED (ANTHROPOCENTRIC) SIMULATION ARGUMENT

In order to overcome some of these issues, I propose a more conservative simulation argument which I call the Anthropocentric Simulation Argument [ASA].[51] Here I assume that *there is only one 'real' human-level civilization in the universe*. The following exposition is intended to show that we do not require the assumption of other base-level civilizations in order to obtain similar results to that of Bostrom's argument.[52] I introduce the following notation:

---

[51] Anthropocentric means that humankind is of the main importance. In this instance I intend for it to mean 'there is only one base level humanlike civilization in the real universe'

[52] Strictly speaking, Bostrom's argument only includes (but does not require) the possibility that we are created by some 'alien' civilization. This is somewhat redundant because if [P3] is true, then we are in a simulation, and whoever created us is, by definition, our 'home' civilization.

P^A – this is the single event probability that we reach a posthuman stage where we run simulations.[53] Where $P^A \in [0,1]$.

N^A – the number of simulations that would be run; $N^A \in \mathbb{N}$.

H^A – the number of human-level observers in our civilization; $H^A \in \mathbb{N}$.

I assume that if we reach a posthuman level, we will run simulations of all of the human-level observers, H^A. The fraction of observers that are simulated therefore is captured by this Anthropocentric Simulation Argument Formula [ASAF]:

$$f_{sim}{}^A = \frac{[P^A N^A H^A]}{[P^A N^A H^A] + H^A} = \frac{[P^A N^A]}{[P^A N^A] + 1}$$

Thus, if we reach a posthuman-level and run simulations ($P^A = 1$), the ASAF becomes:

$$f_{sim}{}^A = \frac{N^A}{N^A + 1}$$

---

[53] The 'A' superscript stands for Anthropocentric. 'P' is to indicate probability of reaching posthumanism.

As before, if we run astronomically large N^A when we become posthuman:[54] $f_{sim}{}^A \to 1$.

The only way for $f_{sim}{}^A = 0$ is if we never run simulations, $P^A = 0$.

The conclusions of my approach are thus slightly different from Bostrom's:

[A1] $P^A = 0$; we do not reach a posthuman stage where we run simulations.
or
[A2] $f_{sim}{}^A \approx 1$; the fraction of all observers that are living in a simulation is near one.

Why do I find the ASAF more appealing? First, the aforementioned 'glitch' is no longer a problem since we do not have to worry about other civilizations that may or may not become posthuman. Second, we are required to make fewer assumptions about things we know nothing about (such as if other humanlike civilizations even exist, and if they do, how many and what kind of simulations they would run). Instead we are working with what we already know about ourselves. And third, we circumvent the associated problems of dealing with

---

[54] Note that we do not even require N^A to be 'astronomically large'. Plugging in example values of 10, 100, 1000 shows that very quickly we will obtain the same result.

infinity and cardinality if we assume that the number of simulations that we run would be finite (although still astronomically large). Most importantly however, we still retain the spirit of Bostrom's conclusion: *the belief that there is a considerable chance that we reach a posthuman level and create ancestor simulations is false, unless we are already in a simulation.*

What would happen, for example, if we reached a posthuman stage imminently? If this is the case, then $P^A = 1$ (we are able to run ancestor simulations). Let us assume that we run simulations of how many individuals are alive right now. H^A would be around 8bn.

The ASAF becomes:

$$f_{sim}{}^A = \frac{N^A\,[8bn]}{N^A\,[8bn] + 8bn} = \frac{N^A}{N^A + 1}$$

As with Bostrom's SAF, H^A factors and cancels out. So, we only need to estimate N^A. How many simulations would we run? This of course depends on the difficulty and the cost of running these simulations. As an interesting proxy, we could perhaps look to the world of life simulation video games, such as *The Sims*.[55] In the last 20 years, this game has sold nearly 200 million copies worldwide, making it one of

---

[55] *The Sims* is an extremely popular video game where you create virtual people (Sims) and essentially have them live out virtual lives by doing things like building houses and starting a family.

the best-selling game franchises of all time (Egenfeldt-Nielsen, 2019: 55). Each time a person brought home the CD and booted it up, a new iteration of The Sims was created. This might be a suitable analogy for what we can expect to happen if we run simulations.[56]

Thus, if the ease of booting up a simulation is analogous to that of running *The Sims* video game, then we can estimate N^A to be something like 200m.

$$f_{sim}{}^A = \frac{[200m]}{[200m] + 1} = \frac{200,000,000}{200,000,001} = 0.999999996.. \cong 1$$

Again, we can capture what is going on with a simple diagram:

---

[56] Of course this is not a perfect approximation because i) the computational requirements of running a PC game for entertainment purposes like *The Sims* game is negligible compared to a real-life simulation, and ii) looking only at the last 20 years is misleading – we would need to consider all of history.

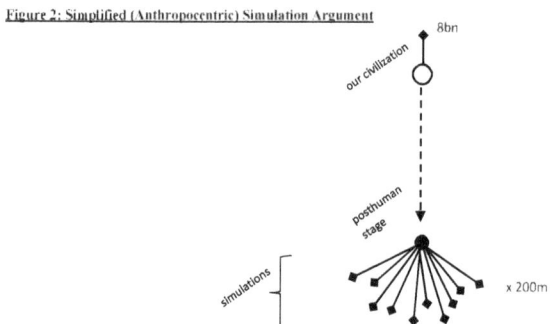

Figure 2: Simplified (Anthropocentric) Simulation Argument

This example is intended to show that we do not necessarily require for there to be other posthuman civilizations in the universe in order to obtain a similar result with regards to the tripartite disjunction. Of course, the possibility of other civilizations that may one day reach a posthuman stage would only cause f_{sim} to increase.

However, this anthropocentric model still has several problems of its own. First, there is an important nuance when we try to use the BIP.[57] Normally, we state that the expectation of being simulated is equal to the fraction of simulated observers over simulated observers plus real observers. But, if we are the ones creating the ancestor simulations, we cannot count those individuals as part of the expectation, because these simulated observers would not contribute towards the chance

---

[57] This was brought to my attention thanks to a comment made by Brian Eggleston (2005).

that we are simulated *since we know we are definitely not them* – because we created them.

Therefore, in our previous example, it would be incorrect to say that *we* have a 0.999999996 chance of being in a simulation, even though that is what we calculated as f_{sim}.[A] What the formula gives us is the probability that *any* randomly picked observer is simulated.[58] We can then say that because we have the ability to run simulations, we are most likely ourselves in a simulation. The reasoning is almost the same as in the original argument: if we are able to create an ancestor simulation, we now have empirical evidence that ancestor simulations are possible. To better understand this, it might help to consider the epistemic situation of someone in one of the simulated universes that we create. Their situation would be exactly the same as ours (apart from the fact that we now know we can create simulations). Therefore, we would need to suspect that we are also in a simulation. [59] One might be tempted to argue: 'but if we are able to run simulations, couldn't we simply be the first generation? Such that all simulated observers have not yet come into existence?' The answer is yes, we could – but what percentage would you assign to that possibility? If we assume that the overall number of simulated observers with human-like experiences is vastly greater than real

---

[58] Note that this is also the case for Bostrom's SAF.

[59] The posthumans that simulated us would have run lots of simulations.

observers (which is outcome [A2] from the ASAF) then we should still believe with high probability that we are amongst the simulated.

Second, there is a question of temporality. If we are able to run simulations, where might we be on the timeline? The answer to this question will affect how we think about the probabilities. Consider the following timeline in the figure below, where we assume that time is linear, and that humanity will reach a posthuman stage where they will run simulations. It is likely that the first simulation will be something of a breakthrough, and there will be some period of time where the simulator is the sole creator of that one simulation.[60]

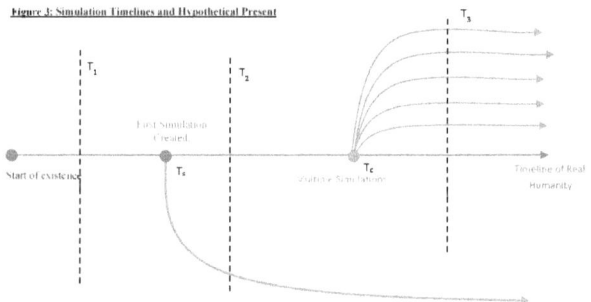

Figure 3: Simulation Timelines and Hypothetical Present

---

[60] There are many reasons why this could be the case: i) power consumption – it could be that the computational requirements are too immense for multiple simulations; ii) financial – it could be too expensive to run many; iii) monopolistic reasons – there is only one person or company that is permitted to run the simulation

We can therefore envisage three different scenarios: i) we are at T_1, which means we are on the real timeline before the first simulation is created – which also means we cannot be simulated; ii) we are at T_2, which is some point after the creation of the first simulation but before many are run. We therefore have a 1 in 2 chance of being in a simulation (if there is only 1 simulation); and iii) we are at T_3, which means we are most likely in a simulation since we are at a point in time when there are many simulations. Herein lies the problem: if we do not know which time we are in, how can we determine our chances of being in a simulation?

Bostrom's argument actually circumvents this problem because he specifies that the simulations are *ancestor* simulations – meaning the timelines would all sprout from the start of existence. Nonetheless, I think this raises even more questions. Would time in the simulation move at the same pace as time in the 'real' world? What happens if a sped-up simulation reaches a posthuman stage? Can you rewind a simulation to a previous time? These are questions that affect both the ASA, and Bostrom's original SA. The analysis in the following section will focus back on Bostrom's original argument and his three outcomes.[61]

---

[61] Unless specific reference is made to the ASAF.

4. INTERPRETATION OF THE SA

If we accept the simulation argument, we then need to ask which one of the three possibilities seems most likely. Bostrom himself doesn't think we have particularly strong evidence for any of them, and therefore we should maybe assign roughly the same probability to each outcome: "in the dark forest of our current ignorance, it seems sensible to apportion one's credence roughly between [1],[2], and [3]" (Bostrom, 2003: 14). In effect, he advocates applying the indifference principle again. If we have three outcomes, and if we have no additional information, then our credence in each epistemic outcome would be 1/3. Here, I strongly disagree, and an analysis of each outcome will show why I think we have stronger reasons to subscribe to the first outcome.

4.1 OUTCOME 1 – ALMOST ALL CIVILIZATIONS FAIL TO REACH A POSTHUMAN STAGE

This outcome can happen for a variety of reasons and it is important to understand the implications of each. Bostrom (2003: 9) notes that, "conditional on [1], we must give a high credence to *DOOM*, the hypothesis that humankind will go extinct before reaching a posthuman level":

$$Cr(DOOM|f_p \approx 0) = 1$$

Which simply means that if the fraction of civilizations that reached a posthuman level is close to zero, our belief should be that we will not reach a posthuman level. However, it is important to note that proposition [1] on its own does not automatically imply that our civilization will die out any time soon. It merely means that we are probably not going to reach a posthuman stage. Often, we face some new existential threat that may change how confident we are about humanity's chances at long term survival. For example, the threat of nuclear war, or something like a more contagious and deadly coronavirus. We cannot rule out that there may be some great filter that prevents us from reaching technological maturity.

I do think that by calling this possibility *DOOM* and stressing the self-destructive aspects of it, Bostrom is somewhat unfairly reducing its credibility.[62] In fact, it seems more commonsensical to think that continued technological progress breaks down and we remain at a stagnant level of development until then eventually becoming extinct (but not because of imminent global catastrophic risk). A more pessimistic possibility is that all technological civilizations collapse, and we go back to a kind of 'dark ages' – and this can happen multiple

---

[62] Although I can understand why he would draw this conclusion given that much of his other work focuses on existential threats and the doomsday scenario (see Bostrom 2019; 2007; 2001)

times.[63] Of course, extinction is an option, but despite Bostrom's obsession with it, it is only one of several.[64] Given that the probability of extinction is unknown, predicated on a plethora of incidentals (the majority of which we cannot know), this is problematic. I have sketched out these four possibilities in Figure 4:

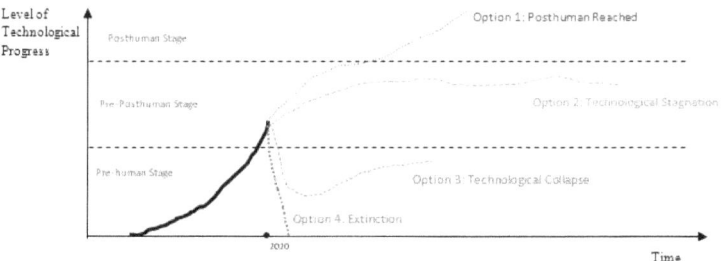

Figure 4: Possible Outcomes for Humanity: *(graph is a schematic and not a strict quantitative representation)*

---

[63] The probability of up and downswings in technological achievements is somewhat of an unknown.

[64] One could argue that Bostrom is justified in that eventually everything (including the stagnated civilization) will indeed come to an end (because of entropy and the heat death of the universe), so perhaps 'extinction' is technically the correct 'catch-all' term, but in that case I would still contest calling the outcome *DOOM*.

Why not call the possibility that we do not reach a posthuman level TECHSTAGNATE? Then,

$$Cr(TECHSTAGNATE|f_p \approx 0) = 1$$

This, to me, seems equally likely (if not more likely) than a doomsday scenario. This would also seem like the most plausible outcome if you are hesitant to accept one or both of Bostrom's initial assumptions. A breakdown in technological progress would of course mean that we will be i) unable to simulate consciousness and ii) lacking the technological capabilities to run simulations. This option, as well as the more pessimistic option of technological collapse, should be given equal credence to that of extinction. In our discussion of the technological assumptions in 2.2, we briefly alluded to the notion of time and how Bostrom's argument stresses the idea that it does not matter *when* we run these simulations. Here I wish to expand on this by once again noting that this is not entirely true because the longer it takes for us to become posthuman, the more likely we are to become extinct. Thus, there is a kind of temporal race between the two outcomes. One could argue that the next few centuries will be a critical phase for humanity which will decide which outcome will prevail (and, ultimately, which of the three disjuncts is true). It is hard to speculate on this because random unpredictable events like a nuclear fallout, or some kind of technological breakthrough in quantum computing would heavily sway the probabilities in different directions.

It is important to note that with Bostrom's argument we should not only be asking what might destroy *us,* but we have to postulate that almost *all human-level civilizations throughout the cosmos* fail to reach technological maturity. If we imagine the universe as containing many more civilizations like ours, then we need to have an answer as to why not a single one of those civilizations was able to reach a level where they would be able to run these simulations. Again, this is highly speculative, and another reason why I prefer the ASAF where we obtain more or less the same outcome without having to guess about the abilities of civilizations that we know nothing about (and it also permits us to carry out the analysis above – which focuses on *our* future trajectories)

4.2 OUTCOME 2: ALL CIVILIZATIONS LOSE INTEREST IN RUNNING SIMULATIONS

[2] $f_I \approx 0$; the fraction of posthumans interested in running a simulation is almost zero.

At the outset, this proposition seems rather peculiar as it would be a drastic departure from the existing situation. Currently, if offered the opportunity to run an ancestor simulation, we would have ample historical and scientific motivations for choosing to do so. For example, historians may be interested to see how a certain alternate history would have turned out.[65] Scientists may be interested in the evolutionary biology of our species. Moreover, the popularity of life-simulation video games like *The Sims* is a strong indicator that there is significant interest in running ancestor simulations.

However, Bostrom argues that we cannot dismiss the possibility that there may be strong reasons in the future as to why this would not happen. For example, it could be that we have ethical reservations about running ancestor simulations (see Jenkins 2006, and Sandberg 2014). Perhaps there is a universal shift in attitudes, and it would be

---

[65] It is a bit strange of Bostrom to assume that future historians would want to re-run *many* simulations of our civilization repeatedly. If they are doing an experiment, we would expect them to have a controlled variation of initial conditions so that they could study different time evolution.

considered horribly unethical to run simulations of conscious people. As a result, there may also be legal ramifications that strictly prohibit ancestor simulations. It could also be that although simulations are possible, it is incredibly expensive or difficult – and for this reason, civilizations decide to use their resources elsewhere.

As before, for [2] to be true, it implies that not just our civilization loses interest in running ancestor simulations, but *all civilizations that reach a posthuman stage* will decide against running ancestor simulations. This must also include individuals within those simulations who may have the resources to be able to do so on their own. Thus, even if there are ten posthuman civilizations with billions of individuals in them, the truth of [2] means that *not a single one* of those individuals with the capability to run ancestor simulations will choose to do so. This is why [2] is also often referred to as the *convergence* hypothesis – because there must be a strong convergence in interests amongst all posthuman civilizations.

This outcome seems exceedingly difficult to envisage not least because we have some good analogous evidence now as to how eager we are to create simulations. Moreover, it is hard to take seriously the notion that simulations will be outlawed and every single posthuman will oblige. We know how easy it is for wealthy individuals to conduct private experiments and research which may not be entirely legal.[66] As aforementioned, speculating on the motivations of these posthuman civilizations is a rather tenuous task. This is why again I prefer to consider the ASAF model where we avoid speculating on the interests of potential posthumans because we group the first two outcomes into [A1] – there will not be any simulations.

---

[66] This can go either way. If simulation technology is treated as something like stem-cell research, then there will of course be independent agents working illegally on developing it because penalties are not that severe. If it is treated as serious as something like nuclear technology, then perhaps not. Also note another caveat: if the simulation is already running and the simulators get caught, it would perhaps be more ethical to let it run even if it is illegal, otherwise you would effectively be committing a sort of mass genocide.

4.3 OUTCOME 3 – WE ARE ALMOST DEFINITELY IN A COMPUTER SIMULATION

The simulation argument purports to show that the disjunction [1] ∨ [2] ∨ [3] is true. If you reject the first two hypotheses, then the third must follow: [3] $f_{sim} \approx 1$; the fraction of all observers in the universe that are living in a simulation is one, and via the BIP, we are almost certainly living in a computer simulation. The strongest piece of evidence in favour of [P3] would be if, for example, tomorrow we were able to run an ancestor simulation (as discussed in the previous section). The only real way we would be able to tell that we were being simulated is if we received some sort of direct sign from our simulators.[67] Besides that, our main source of credence in [P3] would be the refutation of [P1] and [P2] – something that I do not think we have good reason to do.

Although I agree with Bostrom that [P3] is a real possibility, I don't think he is correct to assign it an equal 1/3 credence.[68] Instead, I think

---

[67] Perhaps a large dialogue box could pop up and say, 'YOU ARE LIVING IN A SIMULATION'.

[68] Bostrom has somewhat changed his opinion since the publishing of his paper. On the FAQ page of his website he writes: "Personally, I assign less than 50% probability to the simulation hypothesis – rather something like in 20%-region, perhaps, maybe." https://www.simulation-argument.com/faq.html

we have good empirical reasons for favouring [P1], since it is the outcome that requires the least amount of speculation and additional assumptions. It is the Ockham's Razor of outcomes.[69] This is particularly true if we adopt the less radical, anthropocentric version [A1], where we do not reach a posthuman status not due to some existential threat to humanity, but simply because technological progress stagnates to a point where we are just never able to run the fine-grained highly detailed and conscious simulations that Bostrom envisages. I have tried to capture this idea in the following flowchart (which is made for our civilization, but can be applied across if there are indeed more civilizations with human-level observers):[70]

---

[69] Ockham's Razor tells us that amongst competing possibilities, the one with the fewest assumptions is to be chosen.

[70] This chart is not a fully accurate representation of Bostrom's trilemma because it does not capture the scenario where all three disjuncts could be true at the same time, nor does it take into account the existence of other civilizations and whether they become posthuman.

Figure 5: Simulation Argument – Possibility Flowchart

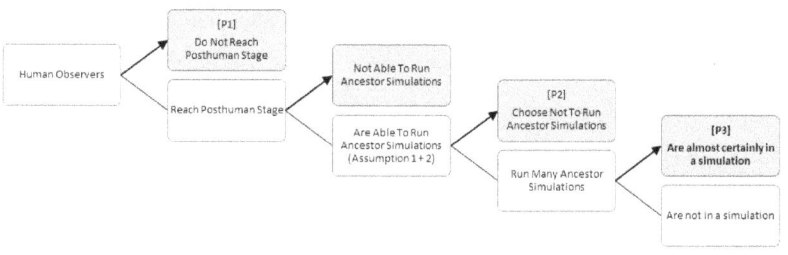

Outcome [P3] rests on a multitude of conditional *if* statements. *If* the assumptions of substrate independence and the assumption of technological feasibility hold; and *if* our posthumans choose to run ancestor simulations with fully conscious human-level observers; and *if* Bostrom's indifference principle is justified. Only then can we say that we *may* be in a simulation (because even then there is still the small statistical chance that we are the 'original').

In contrast, the 'status-quo' version of outcomes is [P1]. If we shift to the anthropocentric version of the simulation argument, then this is even more evident. In order for [A1] to be true, we do not even require the two key assumptions discussed at the start of this book to be true. All that outcome [A1] claims is that *we* do not run ancestor simulations (and we do not need to speculate about the existence of other civilizations in the universe). The average philosophy student unfamiliar with the simulation argument will most likely already hold this view.[71] But, alas, a paper titled *'Are You Going to Technologically Stagnate and Not Reach a Posthuman Stage?'* does not have the same allure as *'Are you Living in a Computer Simulation?'*

---

[71] Of course, this is not to say that this is evidence of it being correct, but it does show that the most likely outcome of Bostrom's paper is probably the least radical.

4.4 A DEPARTURE FROM TRADITIONAL SCEPTICISM

Despite not finding the simulation hypothesis [P3] probable, I do agree with Bostrom that it is fundamentally different from other well-known scepticism scenarios covered in epistemology classrooms. For example, Descartes' evil-demon scenario asks us to imagine that

> […] some malicious demon of the utmost power and cunning has employed all his energies in order to deceive me. […] the sky, the air, the earth, colours, shapes, sounds and all external things are merely delusions of dreams that he has devised to ensnare my judgement.
>
> [Descartes, 1641]

The brain-in-vat scenario offers an updated version of this kind of global Cartesian scepticism, and instead asks the following question: could it be that you and I, and all human beings, are brains in vats? The setup asks us to imagine that we do not have bodies as we think we do, and to instead envisage that we are brains that are floating in nutrient fluid and connected with wires to a supercomputer. Electric impulses are constantly being fed into our brains, and the computer arranges it so that we experience what seems to us the external world.[72] We can then ask the following question: how do you know you are not in this exact scenario right now? In this BIV scenario, we really do *exist*, however, our world is something that is arranged by the computer. Now, imagine a scenario where all sentient beings are these BIVs, and impulses are coordinated so that it seems like we are interacting. This scenario would be qualitatively indistinguishable from the reality that we experience right now, and hence, we could not say with certainty that we are not BIVs.

The simulation argument is significantly different from the BIV argument because it does not ask us to prove the existence of some external world. It instead presents us with a constraint on what we can realistically believe about our universe. This is a sentiment that has been also expressed elsewhere by Chalmers (2003), who argues that the simulation hypothesis is a metaphysical thesis, rather than a radical sceptical one. We do not start from a position of doubt about our external world. Rather, we start by assuming that everything is as it seems, and that science has been a reliable indicator about the nature of our world. Technological progress and developments in neuroscience allow us to say, with some confidence, that in the future we will be able to create ancestor simulations. From this we can deduce that either we do not get to such a stage, or almost all people with our experiences are in simulations. The latter of course is what gives rise to the simulation hypothesis.

---

[72] The external world is the world which exists independent of the mind.

The simulation argument, unlike BIV or Descartes demon's, is a statistical argument. If we were able to envat brains and had empirical reasons to believe that there are *many* envatted brains somewhere out there in the universe, then we would also have statistical reasons to give credence to the BIV scenario. But this is not the case. We do not have any empirical reasons to believe that posthuman civilizations would be interested in envatting and deceiving human brains. We can, however, imagine scenarios where our descendants devote a tiny fraction of their computational resources into running ancestor simulations.

Similarly, if we thought that f_{sim} was relatively small but non-zero (for example, if there were 4 or 5 ancestor simulations), we would not be able to say with confidence that we might be in a simulation. The point of the simulation argument is not to invoke any kind of agnosticism about our world, but rather to make us consider what credence we should assign to each of the three possibilities (one of which is the simulation hypothesis). I do think that Bostrom overstates just how much the simulation argument tells us about the world, especially if, like me, your credence resonates with [P1]. Nonetheless, it would be incorrect to say that the hypothesis that we are in a simulation is as likely or unlikely as the hypothesis that we are a BIV.

The current popularity of Bostrom's argument is most likely due to the fact that the argument is probabilistic in nature. Since it states nothing definitively, it can create an enormous amount of debate and philosophical interest. It is rather unfortunate that when the simulation argument is covered in popular media, it is mischaracterized as 'we might be living in a simulation' or some form of the simulation *hypothesis*. The simulation argument is the disjunct [P1] V [P2] V [P3], and we have shown that despite some issues, the argument is difficult to refute.

4.5 ON TESTING THE SIMULATION HYPOTHESIS

Trying to find evidence that we are not living in a simulation is somewhat of a paradox. There is always the possibility that any evidence that we find is simply a result of the simulator having programmed it to be that way. Nonetheless, there have been several notable studies recently where researchers look for evidence that we might be living in a simulation by trying to see if our simulators somehow 'cut corners' to simplify the simulation. For example, physicists Beane et al. (2012) considered the assumption that with finite computer resources, a simulation would have to be constructed by dividing space-time into discrete data points. They found that some of today's simulations of our universe generate distinct abnormalities — for instance, there are significant tell-tale faults in the behavior of cosmic ray simulations. By observing the cosmic rays, the physicists hinted that we might detect some anomalies, and this can be used as evidence that we live in a simulation. Another paper by Campbell et al. (2017) proposes several experiments that would test the simulation hypothesis. They investigate the assumption that "if the system performing the simulation is finite then to achieve low computational complexity, such a system would, as in a video game, render content (reality) only at the moment that information becomes available for observation by a player and not at the moment of detection by a machine" (Campell et al., 2017: 98). Using this principle, they go on to explain several wave and particle experiments that would be able to test the simulation hypothesis.

In the last few years, several philosophers (see Turchin, 2019; Greene, forthcoming in *Erkenntnis*) have issued warnings about a dangerous paradox involved in discovering whether we live in a simulation or not. If our civilization has been simulated for some sort of research, then one can reasonably deduce that it is important for the simulators that we do not find out that we are in a simulation. If we succeeded in proving that we are simulated, this may very well cause our creators to terminate our simulation.[73] Transhumanist Phil Torres has tried to argue that if we run simulations in the future, we are almost certainly in a nested simulation. Since annihilation is 'inherited downwards', the chance of our simulation getting shut down is rather high, depending on how deep the nesting goes (Torres, 2014). Again, I think this kind of speculation is far-fetched, and not helpful to philosophy nor science. However, I do think that the simulation argument is ripe for further research.

---

[73] In 2017, it was reported by *The New Yorker* that two tech billionaires have 'secretly funded scientists to work on breaking us out of the simulation' if we are indeed in one (Friend, 2017).

5. CONCLUSION

This book has provided a critical assessment of Bostrom's simulation argument. I have shown that although the argument has several issues, many of these are minor and can be overcome by adopting a more conservative formulation. Ultimately, I found that Bostrom's simulation argument is difficult to refute. I then went on to suggest that Bostrom is wrong to assign equal credence to each outcome. Instead, I argued that outcome [P1] should be given preference largely because it requires the least amount of additional assumptions. Finally, I concluded by agreeing with Bostrom that the simulation hypothesis, however unlikely, is fundamentally different from other scepticism scenarios.

REFERENCED READINGS

[1] ASHRAFIAN, H. (20202) 'How Many Simulations Do We Exist In? A Practical Mathematical Solution to the Simulation Argument.' *arXiv preprint arXiv:2001.10439*

[2] BARBEROUSSE, A (2009) "Computer simulations as experiments.' *Synthese* 169.3: 557-574.

[3] BARROW, J.D. (2007) 'Living in a simulated universe.' *Universe or Multiverse?* 481.

[4] BEANE, R., ZOHREH, D., and MARTIN J (2014) 'Constraints on the Universe as a Numerical Simulation.' *The European Physical Journal A* 50.9: 148.

[5] BEISBART, C. (2014) 'Are we sims? how computer simulations represent and what this means for the simulation argument." *The Monist* 97.3: 399-417.

[6] BEREZIN, A. (2007) "Quantum computing and security of information systems." *WIT Transactions on The Built Environment 94*.

[7] BESNARD, F. (2004) 'Refutations of the Simulation Argument.'

[8] BIRCH, J. (2013) 'On the 'Simulation Argument' and Selective Scepticism.' *Erkenntnis* (1975-), vol. 78, no. 1, pp. 95–107.

[9] BOSTROM, N. (1999) 'The doomsday argument is alive and kicking.' *Mind* 108.431: 539-551.

[10] BOSTROM, N. (2001) "The Doomsday argument, Adam & Eve, UN++, and Quantum Joe." *Synthese* 127(3): 359-387

[11] BOSTROM, N. (2002) "Self-locating belief in big worlds: Cosmology's missing link to observation." *The Journal of philosophy* 99.12: 607-623.

[12] BOSTROM, N. (2002b) 'Existential risks: Analyzing human extinction scenarios and related hazards.' *Journal of Evolution and Technology* 9

[13] BOSTROM, N. (2003) 'Are We Living in a Computer Simulation?' *The Philosophical Quarterly*, vol. 53, no. 211, pp. 243–255.

[14] BOSTROM, N. (2005) 'The simulation argument: Reply to Weatherson.' *The Philosophical Quarterly* 55.218 (2005): 90-97.

[15] BOSTROM, N. (2006) 'Why Make a Matrix? And Why You Might Be Living in One.' Chicago: Open Court Publishing.

[16] BOSTROM, N. (2008) 'Why I want to be a posthuman when I grow up.' *Medical enhancement and Posthumanity.* Springer, Dordrecht, 2008. 107-136.

[17] BOSTROM, N. (2009) 'The simulation argument: Some explanations.' *Analysis* 69.3: 458-461.

[18] BOSTROM, N. (2011) 'The simulation argument FAQ.' *Retrieved on 25 June, 2020.*

[19] BOSTROM, N. (2013) 'Existential risk prevention as global priority.' *Global Policy* 4.1: 15-31.

[20] BOSTROM, N. (2019) 'The vulnerable world hypothesis.' *Global Policy* 10.4 (2019): 455-476.

[21] BOSTROM, N. and KULCZYCKI, M. (2011) 'A Patch for the Simulation Argument.' *Analysis*, vol. 71, no. 1, pp. 54–61.

[22] BOSTROM, N. (2010) 'The future of humanity.' *Geopolitics, History, and International Relations*, 1(2), 41–78.

[23] BRADBURY, R. J. (1997) 'Matrioshka Brains.'

[24] BRUECKNER, A. (2008) 'The simulation argument again.' *Analysis* 68.3: 224-226.

[25] CAMPBELL, T. (2017) 'On testing the simulation theory.' arXiv preprint arXiv:1703.00058

[26] CHALMERS, D.J. (1993) 'A computational foundation for the study of cognition.'

[27] CHALMERS, D.J. (2005) 'The matrix as metaphysics.' In Christopher Grau (ed.), *Philosophers Explore the Matrix*. Oxford University Press. pp. 132.

[28] CHALMERS, D.J. (2017) 'The virtual and the real.' *Disputatio* 9.46: 309-352.

[29] ĆIRKOVIĆ, M. (2015) 'Linking simulation argument to the AI risk.' *Futures* 72: 27-31.

[30] CRAWFORD, Lyle. "Freak observers and the simulation argument." *Ratio* 26.3 (2013): 250-264.

[31] CRUMMETT, D. (2020) 'The real advantages of the simulation solution to the problem of natural evil.' *Religious Studies*: 1-16.

[32] DAINTON, B. (2002) 'Innocence lost: simulation scenarios: prospects and consequences.'

[33] DAINTON, B. (2012) 'On singularities and simulations.' *Journal of Consciousness Studies* 19.1-2: 42-85.

[34] DAINTON, B. (forthcoming) 'Natural evil: the simulation solution.' *Religious Studies* 1-22.

[35] DAMASIO, A.R. (1999) *The feeling of what happens: Body and emotion in the making of consciousness*. Houghton Mifflin Harcourt.

[36] DAVIDSON, D. (1970). 'Mental Events', *Essays on Actions and Events*, Oxford: Oxford University Press, 207–223

[37] DAVIES, P. (2004) 'Multiverse cosmological models.' *Modern Physics Letters A* 19.10 727-743.

[38] DENNETT, D. C. (1997) 'Consciousness in Human and Robot Minds' in *Cognition, Computation and Consciousness*, M. Ito, Y. Miyashita and E. T. Rolls (eds.), Oxford: Oxford University Press.

[39] DESCARTES, R, 'Meditations on First Philosophy', in In the Philosophical Writings of Descartes. Volume II, edited by J. Cottingham, 1-62. Cambridge: Cambridge University Press, 1984, p.18.

[40] DREXLER, K. E. (1992) *Nanosystems: Molecular Machinery, Manufacturing, and Computation*, New York, John Wiley & Sons, Inc.,

[41] DREXLER, K.E. (1986) *Engines of Creation*, New York: Anchor Books.

[42] DRINKWATER, B.W. (2020) 'An acoustic black hole.' *Nat. Phys.*

[43] ECKHARDT, W. (2013) 'The Simulation Argument.' *Paradoxes in Probability Theory*. Springer, Dordrecht, 15-17.

[44] EGENFELDT-NIELSEN, D. (2019) *Understanding video games: The essential introduction*. Routledge.

[45] EGGLESTON, B. (2006) 'Review of Bostrom's simulation argument'. Stanford University, https://web.stanford.edu/class/symbsys205/BostromReview.html

[46] FRIEND, T. (2017) "Sam Altman's Manifest Destiny." *The New Yorker*, 2017, www.newyorker.com/magazine/2016/10/10/sam-altmans-manifest-destiny.

[47] GOUVEIA, S. (2020) 'Are we Really Living in a Simulation?' *The Age of Artificial Intelligence: An Exploration*: 145.

[48] GOYAL, S. (2019) 'The Simulation Argument and Incompleteness of Information.' *Vixra*.

[49] GRAU, C. (2005) *Philosophers explore the matrix*. Oxford University Press on Demand.

[50] GRAU, C. (2010) "Bad Dreams, Evil Demons, and the Experience Machine: Philosophy and The Matrix." *Imagine* 17.4.

[51] GREENE, P. (2019). *'Are We Living in a Computer Simulation? Let's Not Find Out.* The New York Times.

[52] GREENE, P. (forthcoming). 'The Termination Risks of Simulation Science.' *Erkenntnis* 1-21.

[53] HAMMARSTROM, A. (2008) *I, Sim - an Exploration of the Simulation Argument* (Thesis), Umea: Umea Universitet.

[54] HANSON, R. (2001) 'How to live in a simulation.' *Journal of Evolution and Technology* 7.1: 3-13.

[55] HAYDEN, E. (2014) 'The $1,000 genome.' *Nature* 507.7492: 294.

[56] IRWIN, W (2002) *The matrix and philosophy: Welcome to the desert of the real.* Vol. 3. Open Court Publishing.

[57] IRWIN, W (2005) *More Matrix and philosophy: Revolutions and Reloaded decoded.* Open Court.

[58] JENKINS, P (2006) 'Historical simulations-motivational, ethical and legal issues.' *Journal of Futures Studies* 11.1: 23-42.

[59] JOHNSON, D.K (2011) 'Natural evil and the simulation hypothesis.' *Philo* 14.2: 161-175.

[60] KARDASHEV, N.S. (1964) "Transmission of information by extraterrestrial civilizations", *Soviet Astronomy*, 8(2).

[61] KIPPING, D. (2020) 'A Bayesian Approach to the Simulation Argument.' Universe 6.8: 109.

[62] KURZWEIL, R. (1999) *The Age of Spiritual Machines: When computers exceed human intelligence*, New York, Viking Press.

[63] LEE, N. (2009) *The Transhumanism Handbook.* Springer Publishing.

[64] LEWIS, P. J. (2013) 'The doomsday argument and the simulation argument.' *Synthese* 190.18: 4009-4022.

[65] LLOYD, S. (2000) 'Ultimate physical limits to computation.' *Nature 406* (31 August):1047-1054

[66] MCDERMOTT, D. (2007). Artificial intelligence and consciousness. *The Cambridge handbook of consciousness*, 117-150.

[67] MITCHELL, J.B. (2020) 'We are probably not Sims.' *Science and Christian Belief.*

[68] MIZRAHI, M (2017) 'The Fine-Tuning Argument and the Simulation Hypothesis.' *Think* 16, no. 46 (2017): 93-102.

[69] MORAVEC, H. (1989). *Mind Children*, Harvard University Press

[70] MORAVEC, H. (1999) *Robot: Mere Machine to Transcendent Mind*, Oxford University Press.

[71] MOSKOWITZ, C (2020) 'Are We Living in A Computer Simulation?'. *Scientific American.*

[72] PENROSE, R. (1971) 'Extraction of rotational energy from a black hole.' Nature Physical Science 229.6: 177-179.

[73] PIGLIUCCI, M. (2013) 'Science & Philosophy: What Hard Problem?' *Philosophy Now* 99: 25-25.

[74] RICHMOND, A. (2017) 'Why doomsday arguments are better than simulation arguments.' *Ratio* 30.3 221-238.

[75] RINGEL, Z., and KOVRIZHIN, D. (2017) 'Quantized gravitational responses, the sign problem, and quantum complexity.' *Science Advances* 3.9: e1701758.

[76] SANDBERG, A. (2008): *Whole Brain Emulation: A Roadmap, Technical Report* #2008-3, Future of Humanity Institute, Oxford University

[77] SANDBERG, A. (2014) "Ethics of brain emulations." *Journal of Experimental & Theoretical Artificial Intelligence* 26.3: 439-457.

[78] SEARLE, J.R. (1984). Can computers think? In *Minds, Brains, and Science*. Cambridge, Mass.: Harvard University Press.

[79] SETH, A. (2009) "The strength of weak artificial consciousness." *International Journal of Machine Consciousness* 1.01 (2009): 71-82.

[80] STEINHART, E. (2010) 'Theological implications of the simulation argument.' *Ars Disputandi* 10.1: 23-37.

[81] STOLJAR, D. (2010). *Physicalism*. Routledge.

[82] TEGMARK, M (2008). 'The mathematical universe.' *Foundations of physics* 38.2: 101-150.

[83] TORRES, P. (2014) 'Why Running Simulations May Mean the End Is Near.' *Institute for Ethics and Emerging*

[84] *Technologies,* ieet.org/index.php/IEET2/more/torres20141103.

[84] TURCHIN, A. (forthcoming). "Simulation Typology and Termination Risks." *arXiv preprint arXiv:1905.05792*

[85] UDLAND, M. (2016) "BANK OF AMERICA: There's a 20%-50% Chance We're inside the Matrix and Reality Is Just a Simulation." Business Insider, Business Insider, 8 Sept. 2016, www.businessinsider.com/bank-of-america-wonders-about-the-matrix-2016-9?r=US&IR=T.

[86] VIRK, R. (2019) *The Simulation Hypothesis: An MIT Computer Scientist Shows Why AI, and Quantum Physics All Agree We Are In A Video Game.* Bayview Books, LLC.

[87] VON BARTHELD CS, B. (2016) The search for true numbers of neurons and glial cells in the human brain: A review of 150 years of cell counting. *J Comp Neurol.*;524(18):3865-3895.

[88] WEATHERSON, B (2003). "Are You a Sim?" *The Philosophical Quarterly* (1950-), vol. 53, no. 212, pp. 425–431.

APPENDIX A: FIXING THE BUG IN THE SIMULATION

If we recall the original equation:

$$f_{sim} = \frac{f_P \, \bar{N} \, \bar{H}}{(f_P \, \bar{N} \, \bar{H}) + \bar{H}}$$

Bostrom and Kulczycki (2011: 2) then ask us to consider the following scenario:

> Imagine a universe in which only two civilizations developed, out of which the first consisted of $3X$ beings and ended without reaching a posthuman stage, while the second reached a posthuman stage after X beings had lived in it, at which point it ran $\bar{N}$ simulations of its ancestral history.

With the above example, $f_P = 0.5$ (since we have 2 civilizations and only one of them reaches a posthuman stage), and $\bar{H} = 2X$ (the average of $3X + X$). Plugging everything in:

$$f_{sim} = \frac{(0.5)\bar{N}(2X)}{(0.5)\bar{N}(2X) + 2X} = \frac{\bar{N}X}{\bar{N}X + 2X} = \frac{\bar{N}}{\bar{N} + 2}$$

The correct fraction however is:

$$\frac{(number\ of\ simulated\ observers)}{(simulated\ observers + real\ observers)} = \frac{\bar{N}X}{\bar{N}X + 3X + X}$$

$$= \frac{\bar{N}X}{\bar{N}X + 4X} = \frac{\bar{N}}{\bar{N} + 4}$$

We are getting a discrepancy because of how the formula relies on taking an average number ($\bar{H}$) of observers from both, when in reality we should only be focused on those that reach a posthuman stage (since they will be the ones running simulations). Note however that as long as $\bar{N}$ is sufficiently large (in this example, even $\bar{N} > 100$ will suffice), this does not really impact the result. We assume that there will be large amounts of simulations run.

Bostrom then goes on to describe an even more radical example, which can be obtained by carefully choosing more extreme numbers:

> Consider there is one civilization in which $99(99\bar{N} - 1)X$ people lived, and which never reached a posthuman stage. In addition, there are 99 civilizations that reached a posthuman stage after X people lived in each of them. Assume that each of those 99 civilizations run $\bar{N}$ simulations of its entire ancestral history.
>
> [Bostrom and Kulczycki, 2011: 2]

Thus, we have 100 civilizations in total, 99 of which manage to reach a posthuman stage. Therefore $f_P = 0.99$. All the posthuman civilizations are interested in running ancestor simulations, which means that $f_I = 1$.

Recall the [SAF]:

$$f_{sim} = \frac{f_P f_I \bar{N}}{(f_P f_I \bar{N}) + 1}$$

Plugging in what we know,

$$f_{sim} = \frac{(0.99)(1)\bar{N}}{[(0.99)(1)\bar{N}] + 1}$$

$$= \frac{\bar{N}}{\bar{N} + \frac{100}{99}}$$

For large $\bar{N}$, the f_{sim} will tend towards 1, and this suggests that everyone is in a simulation.

When in truth the fraction should really be:

$$\frac{(number\ simulated\ observers)}{(simulated\ observers + real\ observers)}$$

$$= \frac{99\ \bar{N}X}{99\ \bar{N}X + 99(99\bar{N} - 1)X + 99X} = \frac{\bar{N}}{\bar{N} + 99\bar{N}}$$

$$= \frac{1}{100}$$

Clearly this result is problematic for Bostrom's disjunction because we now have the following:

$f_P = 0.99$; [almost all civilizations reached a posthuman level].

$f_I = 1$; [all posthuman civilizations were interested in running ancestor simulations].

$f_{sim} = 0.01$; [almost nobody is in a simulation].

This would seem to indicate that all three of Bostrom's propositions are simultaneously false, and the whole simulation argument is therefore compromised.[74] It is evident from these examples that the fundamental problem is caused by *instances where the average*

---

[74] It should be noted that this example is very strange in the sense that one of the simulations population was expressed in terms of the number of simulations run ($\bar{N}$). The authors likely did this on purpose so the $\bar{N}$ would cancel out in the equation to make their point.

number of people living in the pre-posthuman phase is significantly different in civilizations do not produce ancestor simulation than from those that do.

Bostrom & Kulczycki (2011) propose at least three ways to deal with this vulnerability, one of which I outline here. This method requires an additional assumption to ensure that the "typical duration (or more precisely, the typical cumulative population) of the pre-posthuman phase *does not differ by an astronomically large factor* between civilizations that never run a significant number of ancestor simulations and those that eventually do" (Bostrom & Kulczycki, 2011: 3, emphasis in original). So, what exactly is an astronomically large factor? We will now show that Bostrom's key disjunct can be obtained even when we assume that the difference in populations is set to a factor of *one million*.

Let us denote the civilizations that are definitely running simulations with an s, such that there have been s civilizations that run $\overline{N}$ ancestor simulations. The average number of observers (pre-posthuman) in them is then H_s. There are also n civilizations that do not reach a posthuman status. The average number of observers in those civilizations is H_n. Bostrom and Kulczycki (2011) then implement the following constraint:[75]

---

[75] Which just means that the *difference in populations is less than one million.*

[C1]
$$1{,}000{,}000 \cdot H_n \leq \overline{N} \cdot H_s$$

Or alternatively,

[C2]
$$\frac{H_n}{H_s} \leq \frac{\overline{N}}{1{,}000{,}000}$$

Which simply means that the difference in pre-posthuman population size of the civilization that does not reach posthuman status is no greater than one million times that of the pre-posthuman population of civilizations that do reach posthuman status and are able to run N simulations of their ancestral history.

We can also work out exactly how many 'real' observers there are by simply multiplying the average number of observers in each category by the number of civilizations there are of that category:

$$nH_n + sH_s = [real\ beings]$$

We do not know exactly how many simulated beings there will be (because perhaps not all posthuman civilizations will be interested in running ancestor simulations) but we know it is *at least* $\overline{N} \cdot s \cdot H_s$

(because s is the amount of posthuman civilizations that definitely run simulations and not all posthuman civilizations will run simulations).

Our Simulation Argument Formula therefore is, [76]

$$f_{sim} \geq \frac{simulated}{simulated + [real]}$$

Plugging in the above,

$$f_{sim} \geq \frac{\bar{N}sH_s}{\bar{N}sH_s + [nH_n + sH_s]}$$

If we factor out NsH_s,

$$f_{sim} \geq \frac{\bar{N}sH_s}{\bar{N}sH_s \left[1 + \frac{nH_n}{\bar{N}sH_s} + \frac{sH_s}{\bar{N}sH_s}\right]}$$

Cancelling variables out,

---

[76] The $\geq$ is the mathematical equivalent of 'at least', which we want because we know that if some civilizations choose to simulate, that will make the RHS smaller (multiplying by a fraction).

$$f_{sim} \geq \frac{1}{1 + \frac{nH_n}{\bar{N}sH_s} + \frac{1}{\bar{N}}}$$

Bringing out $\frac{1}{\bar{N}}$ in the denominator,

$$f_{sim} \geq \frac{1}{1 + \frac{1}{\bar{N}}\left[1 + \frac{n}{s}\frac{H_n}{H_s}\right]}$$

If we substitute for $\frac{H_n}{H_s}$ from [C2],

[C2] $\frac{H_n}{H_s} \leq \frac{\bar{N}}{1,000,000}$

$$f_{sim} \geq \frac{1}{1 + \frac{1}{\bar{N}}\left[1 + \frac{n}{s}\frac{H_n}{H_s}\right]}$$

$$f_{sim} \geq \frac{1}{1 + \frac{1}{\bar{N}}\left[1 + \frac{n}{s}\frac{\bar{N}}{1,000,000}\right]}$$

We recall that we need $f_{sim} \geq 0.99$ in order for [3] to hold.

To see what happens if $f_{sim} < 0.99$:

$$\frac{1}{1+\frac{1}{\bar{N}}\left[1+\frac{n}{s}\frac{\bar{N}}{1,000,000}\right]} < \frac{99}{100}$$

Flipping everything over

$$\frac{100}{99} < 1+\frac{1}{\bar{N}}\left[1+\frac{n}{s}\frac{\bar{N}}{1,000,000}\right]$$

Simplifying,

$$\frac{1}{99}-\frac{1}{\bar{N}} < \frac{n}{s \cdot 1,000,000}$$

We made the earlier assumption that there would be a large number of simulations, therefore we know that $\bar{N}$ is large. If $\bar{N} > 9900$, we have[77]

$$\frac{1}{99}-\frac{1}{\bar{N}} > \frac{1}{99}-\frac{1}{9900} = \frac{1}{100}$$

Substituting back,

$$\frac{1}{100} < \frac{n}{s \cdot 1,000,000}$$

---

[77] Bostrom and Kulczycki choose '9900' simply because it makes the result of the subsequent calculation more convenient (in that we get a nice fraction – 1/100)

Simplifying,

$$s \cdot 1{,}000{,}000 < 100 \cdot n$$

$$s \cdot 10{,}000 < n$$

This indicates that for every civilization running $\overline{N}$ simulations we will have at minimum 10,000 civilizations that do not.

Bostrom and Kulczycki (2011: 6) then propose we introduce some notation to indicate civilizations that are posthuman but not interested in running simulations. Let $n = a + b$ where a is the *amount of civilizations* that do not achieve posthuman stage, and b is the *amount of civilizations* that do achieve posthuman stage but *choose not to run simulations* (or choose not to run a significant amount of simulations, fewer than N).

Then we can show that if $b \geq 99 \cdot s$ the second statement of the tripartite ([2] $f_I \approx 0$) will hold because any civilization that is posthuman will be less than 1% likely to run ancestor simulations.

We can also see what happens if $b < 99 \cdot s$

$$s \cdot 10{,}000 < a + b$$

Subbing in for *b*,

$$s \cdot 10{,}000 < a + 99 \cdot s$$

Simplifying,

$$9901 \cdot s < a$$

Which indicates that for every civilization running simulations, there will be more than 9900 civilizations that fail to reach a posthuman stage.

Bostrom and Kulczycki (2011: 6) thus arrive at the following conclusions:

1. s civilizations reach post-humanity and run $\bar{N}$ simulations
2. Less than $99s$ civilizations reach a post-human stage but run less than $\bar{N}$ simulations
3. There are at least $9900s$ civilizations that fail to reach post-human stage

We can also work the fraction of civilizations that never reach the post-human stage:

$$\frac{9900}{9990 + 99 + 1} = 0.99$$

Therefore [3] $f_{sim} \approx 1$, also holds true.

This exercise has shown that even with a difference factor of one million (between civilizations that do run simulations and those that do not), we are able to retain Bostrom's trilemma and avoid the glitch. How plausible is this additional constraint? Bostrom and Kulczycki (2011) suggest that we look at our own civilization to see if this is realistic. We are pre-posthuman, and there have been roughly 110bn 'observers' in our civilization. In order for the assumption to fail, other civilizations in our universe that reach a posthuman status but do not run a significant amount of simulations would need to have in excess of *100 million billion* pre-posthuman observers. Thus, the assumption is probably a rather realistic one. However, given how it can impact the key tripartite proposition, it is not unimportant.[78]

---

[78] For numerical solutions to the simulation argument that incorporate these 'fixes', see Ashrafian (2020) and Goyal (2019). Kipping (2020) uses a Bayesian approach to the simulation argument.

APPENDIX B: USING DENSITIES FOR AN INFINITE UNIVERSE

We can use the idea of limit density to accommodate the possibility of an infinite universe.[79] First, we pick some arbitrary point, P, in spacetime.

Then we draw around it a hypersphere with radius R.

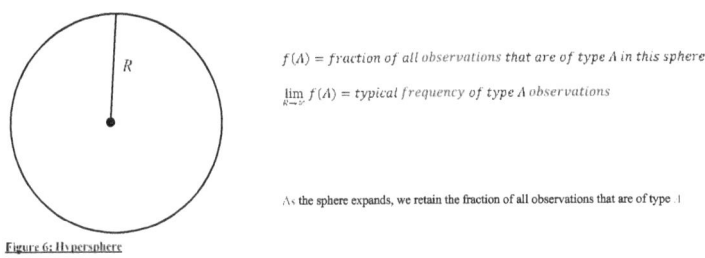

$f(A)$ = fraction of all observations that are of type A in this sphere

$\lim_{R \to \infty} f(A)$ = typical frequency of type A observations

As the sphere expands, we retain the fraction of all observations that are of type A

Figure 6: Hypersphere

Bostrom suggests that we can use this basic idea for the simulation argument. We would first need to define the original point as some location in the base level of reality (where the computer running our simulation is located). Then we can take this expansion of the hypersphere from that level. The central idea here is if we can capture the situation (in terms of f_p, f_I, f_{sim}) for a slice of the universe (and note the *observable* universe is finite; however only a small part of the universe is observable by us), we can extrapolate that across an

---

[79] This solution was inspired by a comment made by Bostrom on his website: https://www.simulation-argument.com/faq.html

infinite universe. Of course, there is no guarantee that the slice of the universe we are observing has the same corresponding density as an infinitely expanding universe.

APPENDIX C: EXAMINER FEEDBACK

Some Positives:

This dissertation is exemplary in its clarity, structure, scholarship and the acumen of its arguments. The literature on this topic, namely the likelihood that we're living in a computer simulation, spans a number of areas, e.g. philosophy, physics and cognitive science, and the student has done admirably in conveying some of the nuances present in the discussions that have emerged in those areas. This includes mathematical and physical nuances. The topic is obviously well-researched and the student even provides some additional sections in the form of appendices that go into some technical issues, should the reader wish to follow up on them. Overall, a very impressive job indeed.

Some Negatives:

I have doubts about the student's own formulation of the argument (which they call 'ASA'). Contrary to what the student seems to suggest, there is still considerable speculation involved in this argument. Future and even counterfactual probabilities and quantities like the number of simulations that we would run were we to reach a post-human stage don't appear to be any easier to calculate than the quantities involved in Bostrom's argument. Moreover, if it is possible that we are being simulated, that means that the relevant probability we need to take into account when calculating the probability that any given individual is a real or simulated one is not the probability that we will run simulations at some point in the future but rather the more general probability that some relevant class of civilisations will run simulations at some point in the future. That's because the latter probability covers also the cases where we are being simulated by other (similar-in-some-respects) civilisations. Indeed, the relevance of a broader class of civilisations becomes even more pressing when one takes into account the view that simulations may be performed by civilisations on other, i.e. alien, civilisations. This would make total sense if one is running these simulations for scientific purposes. It's not clear why the student thinks that the number of assumptions made makes a difference to whether or not a given scenario is probable? Does it not matter what these assumptions assert? Is it the case that P1 implies (a version of) P2 but not vice-versa? If so P1 can be thought of as the conjunction of P2 and some other content. But the probability of a conjunction is equal to or less to the probability of each individual conjunct. Thus, P1 is less likely than P2 on this rationale. Other issues include: A disjunction is not an argument but a claim. What you presumably mean is that Bostrom uses other claims to support the conclusion that at least one of the three main claims is true. For example, if one shows that the two disjuncts are false, then the last disjunct can be derived as a conclusion. That's an argument.

Viva:

The student did well in the viva and clearly demonstrated that he was in control of the subject matter. He gave a very good overview of the dissertations and responded well to questions. Some of the questions posed by the examiners remained unanswered, e.g. the question about Williamson's objection and how it affects the indifference principle, but those questions were by and large difficult and on material that the student was not expected to have read. The student offered some thoughtful answers to the objection that the computer simulation hypothesis is just another sceptical hypothesis, pointing out that the former is supported by a statistical argument whereas typical sceptical hypothesis are not. In reply to the follow-up objection that the latter can in principle be supported by statistically formulated arguments, the student argued that it's hard to motivate the claim that a civilisation would start envatting brains, whereas it's easier to motivate the claim that they would start running computer simulations. The punchline being that statistical versions of the arguments that support brain-in-a-vat or similar hypotheses seem unnecessary.

www.ingramcontent.com/pod-product-compliance
Lightning Source LLC
Chambersburg PA
CBHW070044230426
43661CB00005B/745